Great Crosswords for Kids

Trip Payne

PUZZLE WRIGHT PRESS

An imprint of Sterling Publishing Co., Inc.

www.puzzlewright.com

Dedicated to my sister, Peggy Payne,
even though I was the only kid in the family
who was a fan of crossword puzzles.

Puzzlewright Press and the distinctive Puzzlewright Press logo are
registered trademarks of Sterling Publishing Co., Inc.

16   18   20   19   17   15

Published by Sterling Publishing Company, Inc.
387 Park Avenue South, New York, N.Y. 10016
© 2002 by Trip Payne
Distributed in Canada by Sterling Publishing
℅ Canadian Manda Group, 165 Dufferin Street
Toronto, Ontario, Canada M6K 3H6
Distributed in the United Kingdom by GMC Distribution Services
Castle Place, 166 High Street, Lewes, East Sussex, England BN7 1XU
Distributed in Australia by Capricorn Link (Australia) Pty. Ltd.
P.O. Box 704, Windsor, NSW 2756 Australia

Manufactured in the United States of America
All rights reserved

Sterling ISBN 978-0-8069-9289-1

For information about custom editions, special sales, premium
and corporate purchases, please contact Sterling Special Sales
Department at 800-805-5489 or specialsales@sterlingpublishing.com

CONTENTS

INTRODUCTION

These puzzles are filled with things you know—books you've read, games you've played, foods you like to eat, stuff like that. There aren't any really weird things in here that sometimes show up in crossword puzzles that grown-ups do, like ancient French coins and rare African antelopes.

But there are probably a few words here and there that you won't know. That's okay! Maybe you can figure them out from the words that cross them. Or maybe you can ask someone—a friend or a parent or someone. And once you find out what those words are, you'll be ready for them the next time you see them in a puzzle!

Happy puzzling!

—Trip Payne

PUZZLES

1

ACROSS

1 Island country near Florida
5 Melt
9 Sticky stuff
12 A ___ apple: 2 words
13 Car
14 It might be pierced
15 Hairless
16 Member of the singing Chipmunks
18 Where Santa invites kids to sit
20 "Oh, ___ Pete's sake!"
21 One of the Seven Dwarfs
23 Direction where the sun rises
27 Assistant to Dr. Frankenstein
30 Sick
31 How you say "hello" and "goodbye" in Hawaii
33 Female sheep
34 Work for a newspaper or magazine
36 Cain's brother, in the Bible
37 Marry
38 At this very moment
40 Where a scientist works
42 "Batman" villain who says words like "purrrr-fect"
47 Light ___ (item in a lamp)
50 A long time ___ (in the past)
51 Red flower with sharp thorns
52 The world's largest continent
53 Ballpoint ___
54 Beef or pork, for example
55 All of those people

DOWN

1 Taxi
2 Its capital is Washington, D.C.: Abbreviation
3 He became president in 1993: 2 words
4 Cost an arm ___ leg: 2 words
5 "I tawt I taw a puddy ___!" (Tweety's saying)
6 "What did you say?"
7 Had a meal
8 Sound of a dog's bark
9 He became president in 2001: 3 words
10 It's used to paddle a canoe
11 State that's north of California: Abbreviation
17 "Where ___ go from here?": 2 words

19 Little vegetable found in a pod

21 Opposite of "live"

22 ___ Maid (card game)

24 Pie ___ mode (dessert with ice cream): 2 words

25 Cry

26 Jack-in-___-box

28 "I ___ you one!" ("Thanks for the help!")

29 One of the colors on the American flag

32 "Th-th-that's ___, folks!" (words from Porky)

35 Drag a car off the side of the road

39 Wiggly animal that you might use as fishing bait

41 Blind as ___: 2 words

42 What a baseball player wears on the head

43 How old a person is

44 One of the Three Stooges

45 Quiet ___ mouse: 2 words

46 It's in the middle of a tennis court

48 Say something that isn't true

49 Green ___ Packers (pro football team)

7

2

ACROSS

1 Used a chair
4 Agency that sends people into space: Abbreviation
8 Soup comes in these containers
12 "You ___ My Sunshine"
13 "That's just the way ___": 2 words
14 Kid on "The Andy Griffith Show"
15 False statement
16 Expensive property in the game Monopoly: 2 words
18 Puts in the mail
20 Long-___ (like Bugs Bunny)
21 Not to mention
22 Soft drink
25 Make an effort
26 ___ checkers (game with marbles)
29 ___ up (drink like a dog)
32 "Planet of the ___"
33 Cards that can be worth either 1 or 11 in blackjack
37 Edgar ___ Poe (famous American writer)
39 It holds a purse around a woman's shoulder
40 Expensive property in the game Monopoly

44 "What's the ___?" ("It doesn't matter anyway")
45 "Step ___!" ("Hurry!"): 2 words
46 Do as you're told
47 Christmas is in this month: Abbreviation
48 Baseball team from Cincinnati
49 What people catch butterflies in
50 Animal with large antlers

DOWN

1 You might dip nachos in this sauce
2 Name of the mermaid in "The Little Mermaid"
3 People older than 12 but younger than 20
4 Itty-bitty bites
5 "Now ___ theater near you!" (movie ad phrase): 2 words
6 What a private calls a sergeant, in the army
7 "___ a silly question, get a silly answer!"
8 Coke or Pepsi, for example
9 "I can't tell them ___" ("They look the same")

Crossword Grid

Clues

10 More pleasant
11 Like the inside of a watermelon
17 Round green vegetables
19 Friend of Sleepy and Grumpy
22 Drink through a straw
23 Word on a penny
24 ___ Moines (capital of Iowa)
27 You ball it up to make a fist
28 Have lunch
29 ___ Day (holiday in early September)
30 Without anyone else around
31 Clothing pattern that has different colors crossing each other
34 Gross, like belching at the table
35 Stand that's used to hold up a painting
36 Little bit of dust or soot
38 Martial ___ (karate, judo, etc.)
39 "The ___ the limit!" ("We can do anything!")
41 Took first place
42 Nickname for President Lincoln
43 Allow

3

ACROSS

1 Batman and Superman wear them
6 "To boldly go where no man ___ gone before" ("Star Trek" line)
9 It's similar to jelly
12 Ring ___ (sound familiar): 2 words
13 Covered with frozen water
14 Long ___ (in the past)
15 Soft drink that competes with Coke
16 "Yes, ___" (way to agree with a man)
17 "Charlotte's ___" (book about a spider)
18 Name of a skunk in some cartoons
20 Stupid
22 Part of the foot
24 Opposite of "happy"
26 A woman might carry her money and makeup in it
29 Dumbo flapped these in order to fly
31 "You can't have your cake and eat it ___"
33 Hand out the cards
34 Metal suit worn by a knight
36 One of Santa's assistants

38 Cash machine outside a bank: Abbreviation
39 "Peekaboo, ___ you!": 2 words
41 A teacher sits behind one
43 Frying ___ (kitchen item)
45 What Noah built
47 Requires
50 Have a part in a play
51 "Cross my heart and hope to ___"
52 Christmas ___ (kind of song you hear in December)
53 It isn't "no" or "maybe"
54 Money used in Japan
55 "What I Did on My Summer Vacation," for example

DOWN

1 "Put on your thinking ___!"
2 Name of Bart Simpson's grandfather
3 Hard candies
4 "Or ___!" (part of a threat)
5 Stumbles
6 Not hers

10

7 Dangerous liquid found inside batteries

8 You pour it on pancakes

9 Hard candies

10 "Act your ___ and not your shoe size!"

11 Crowd of people

19 Chow down

21 Pigs roll around in it

22 Drink that's popular in China

23 It makes a canoe move

25 Female deer

27 Stopped standing

28 Kind of tree

30 Letters that mean "help me!"

32 Ancient

35 "___ or not, here I come!"

37 It might surround a yard

40 One of the five Great Lakes

42 Large bodies of water

43 ___ attention (listen carefully)

44 "___ Ventura, Pet Detective"

46 Barbie's friend

48 "___ good turn daily" (Boy Scout slogan): 2 words

49 ___ as a fox (very sneaky)

4

ACROSS

1 Gets older
5 It might be parked in a garage
8 Touches softly
12 "Pleased to ___ you!"
13 "It's no ___!" ("It won't work!")
14 Thought
15 Large body of water on the east coast of America: 2 words
18 Part of the body that has a nail
19 Liquid inside a pen
20 Opposite of "hired"
23 Big relative of a monkey
24 Month before June
27 Cards that are sometimes better than kings
28 Dessert that has a crust
29 Opening in a fence
30 Homer's neighbor, on "The Simpsons"
31 Container for jelly
32 Squares of glass in a window
33 "___ Got the Whole World in His Hands"
34 What's on the skin of a bear or cat
35 Large body of water in Utah: 3 words
42 Incorrect way to say "isn't"

43 Christmas ___ (December 24)
44 Flower that has the same name as a part of the eye
45 Peas grow in them
46 Mediterranean ___ (large body of water)
47 Penny

DOWN

1 "I ___ bear of very little brain" (Winnie-the-Pooh quote): 2 words
2 "___ out of here!" ("Leave!")
3 Long, skinny fish
4 United ___ of America
5 Adorable
6 "Do ___ tell you!": 2 words
7 List of instructions that a cook follows
8 Choose
9 It can follow "lemon" or "Gator" in names of drinks
10 Beverage made by Lipton
11 ___ Francisco, California
16 Wynken, Blynken, and ___ (characters in a poem)
17 Nine minus eight

20 ___ mail (letters sent to famous people)

21 Cubes you can find in a freezer

22 Main color of a stop sign

23 People breathe it

24 Grown-up boy

25 Had a snack

26 "Uh-huh"

28 Doesn't fail a class in school

29 Food that can make your breath stink

31 Fast airplane

32 "I can't ___ up with this any longer!"

33 "The 500 ___ of Bartholomew Cubbins" (Dr. Seuss book)

34 Little insect that might bother a dog

35 Space between two teeth

36 ___ Grande (Texas river)

37 From beginning to ___

38 Illinois ___ (space in Monopoly): Abbreviation

39 "Just who do you think you ___?"

40 Family members

41 Ending for "small" that makes it mean "most small"

5

ACROSS

1 The fourth planet from the sun
5 Does a dance that makes "click" sounds with the shoes
9 Hobo
12 Bunches: 2 words
13 Continent where India is
14 Pretty ___ picture: 2 words
15 What day, month, and year it is
16 Dr. Seuss book: 2 words
18 You wipe your feet on it before entering a house
20 Room that might have a TV
21 One of the Bobbsey Twins
24 "You're ___ the boss of me!"
26 You twist these in order to open some bottles
30 Dr. Seuss book: 3 words
34 Hit a ___ (run into problems)
35 Brown beverage
36 Animal in a dairy
37 Fuel for a car
40 A vain person might have a big one
42 Dr. Seuss book: 3 words

46 ___ Le Pew (cartoon skunk)
50 Lamb's mother
51 Dial ___ (sound you hear on the phone)
52 Like the numbers 2, 4, and 6
53 What you hit a badminton birdie over
54 Part of a constellation
55 Geeky person

DOWN

1 Magazine featuring Alfred E. Neuman
2 State next to Georgia: Abbreviation
3 Decay
4 Long, skinny part of a flower
5 Art on a person's skin
6 One of the Pokémon trainers
7 The ___ Piper of Hamelin
8 When a store lowers its prices
9 Candy ___ (sweet treat)
10 The country south of Canada: Abbreviation
11 The Grinch's pet dog
17 "___ upon a time ..."

19 "Baa baa black sheep, have you ___ wool?"

21 They aren't yeses

22 Raggedy ___ (kind of doll)

23 Michael Jordan's sports organization: Abbreviation

25 It causes explosions: Abbreviation

27 Start of the alphabet

28 Athlete who gets paid

29 Carpenter's cutting tool

31 Brand of frozen waffles

32 Further away from the shallow end of the pool

33 Zig and ___

38 Insects that like picnics

39 "X marks the ___" (treasure map's phrase)

41 Not closed

42 "The Little Red ___" (story)

43 What the O in I.O.U. stands for

44 Dog, cat, or hamster, for example

45 Go ___ diet (try to lose weight): 2 words

47 Adam's wife, in the Bible

48 Miles ___ hour (how a car's speed is measured)

49 Finish

6

ACROSS

1 Pierce with a knife
5 Ring of flowers you put around your neck in Hawaii
8 "I have an idea!"
11 "Who Wants ___ a Millionaire": 2 words
12 Sudden surprise
13 Easy as falling off a ___
14 "That won't do you ___ of good!": 2 words
15 Does something with
16 ___ of these days (sometime soon)
17 Enters, as a car: 2 words
19 ___ potatoes and gravy
21 Part of your body that includes the pupil
22 Green fruit
24 Horses eat it
25 George ___ (star of the movie "Batman & Robin")
27 Unhappy
29 Goes bad
30 Covered with water
33 "___ and the Amazing Technicolor Dreamcoat"
35 "Things are not always what they ___ to be"
37 Deer with large antlers
38 Someone who isn't telling the truth
40 Give a grade to
41 New Year's ___ (December 31)
42 Not beautiful
43 A chef bakes things in it
44 Color of a ripe tomato
45 That woman
46 Fix, as socks

DOWN

1 The part of a theater where the actors are
2 ___ Maguire (star of the movie "Spider-Man")
3 Have ___ to eat (snack on something): 2 words
4 Gambles
5 ___ Angeles, California
6 Kind of school
7 "___ small world after all": 2 words
8 How you say "hello" in Honolulu

16

9 Bees make it
10 Turned another year older
12 Kind of school: 2 words
18 Its capital is Springfield: Abbreviation
20 A little nervous about meeting new people
23 Sound you might hear in a dairy
25 Letters between B and F
26 Supposed ability to read minds: Abbreviation

27 Complete a crossword puzzle
28 Said a question
30 Make a potholder, for example
31 Devoured
32 Something so popular that everyone seems to be doing it
33 Make fun of
34 What " + " means
36 Formal dance that older students go to
39 Ginger ___ (kind of drink)

7

ACROSS

1 Dog's hand
4 Jack and ___
8 Pieces of wood that are put in a fireplace
12 Country between Canada and Mexico: Abbreviation
13 Dog in the comic strip "Garfield"
14 "___ what you mean" ("That makes sense"): 2 words
15 Bird that can be taught to talk
17 Food that contains meat, potatoes, and other vegetables
18 "The Princess and the ___" (fairy tale)
19 Rip
21 You might use it to keep wrapping paper in place
24 State whose capital is Carson City: Abbreviation
25 What the bride and groom say to the priest: 2 words
28 It keeps your drink cold
29 Be ___ of (know about)
31 Pro and ___ (sides in a debate)
32 It's filled with ink
33 Where you put your napkin when you eat

34 "There was an old woman who lived in a ___"
35 Tiger Woods plays this sport
37 ___-tac-toe
39 Twirled around
41 Pink bird with long legs
46 Name of the prince in "The Little Mermaid"
47 Where Aladdin's genie lived
48 ___ and arrow (what you use in archery)
49 Dial ___
50 Parts of the face
51 Had some food

DOWN

1 Young dog
2 White ___ sheet: 2 words
3 Card game for two people
4 It ends with a punch line
5 Thought
6 "I cannot tell a ___"
7 You put it in an envelope
8 One of Bart Simpson's sisters
9 The largest bird in the world
10 "___ whiz!"

11 Use a needle and thread

16 Bigger relative of a monkey

20 Adam and ___

21 Money that's left for the waiter

22 Card with a single spot on it

23 Black-and-white bird

24 Sleep for a little while

26 Scooby-___

27 "___ nation under God, indivisible ..." (part of the Pledge of Allegiance)

29 Everything

30 Square breakfast food

34 Biology or physics, for example: Abbreviation

36 ___ in a while (sometimes)

37 Not wild

38 Bratty kids

39 "Ready, ___, go!"

40 Athlete who isn't an amateur

42 "Now I ___ me down to sleep ..."

43 The Los Angeles Lakers are in this group: Abbreviation

44 "You've ___ to be kidding!"

45 Have debts

8

ACROSS

1 Without any clothes on
5 I ___ (game where you try to see something)
8 Sound made by a ray gun
11 Gorillas
12 "That's ___ bad!"
13 "... and a partridge ___ pear tree": 2 words
14 Magazine for young children: 2 words
17 Sports group that uses pucks: Abbreviation
18 P. Diddy's music
19 What cows say
22 Name of a cartoon cat from the 1990s
24 Butter ___ (ice cream flavor)
28 Piece of jewelry you wear on the hand
30 Stop standing
32 Three-legged ___ (picnic event)
33 Kind of winter weather
35 "What ___ you say?" ("Huh?")
37 Animal you keep at home
38 Positive answer
40 "It's ___ fair!"
42 Magazine for young children: 2 words
48 "___ Been Working on the Railroad"
49 Have to pay money to
50 "As I was going to St. Ives, I met ___ with seven wives": 2 words
51 Miles ___ gallon (what MPG stands for)
52 Stuff that makes hair stiff
53 Make a shot in miniature golf

DOWN

1 "___, humbug!" (what Scrooge said)
2 Convenience store worker on "The Simpsons"
3 Rock band that sang "Shiny Happy People"
4 Cable channel that shows sports: Abbreviation
5 Ways to arrange your hair
6 It holds peas
7 "What's ___ name?"
8 You use it to open a sleeping bag
9 Little insect
10 ___ attention (listen carefully)
15 "Beauty and ___ Beast"
16 It shows you how to get from one place to another

19 "___ Doubtfire" (movie comedy starring Robin Williams)

20 What Dorothy used to make the Tin Man move again

21 "... and ___ to grow on" (birthday saying)

23 Baby goat

25 "Stuck a feather in his ___ and called it macaroni" (line from "Yankee Doodle")

26 Card with an A in the corner

27 It's in the middle of a Ping-Pong table

29 Old Faithful is a famous one

31 Shiny stuff you put on a Christmas tree

34 Iced ___ (cold drink)

36 Wakko and Yakko's sister on "Animaniacs"

39 Polluted air

41 It might catch a mouse

42 Take a little drink

43 The first woman, according to the Bible

44 Lamb's mother

45 Big bird from Australia

46 Have supper

47 Explosive stuff: Abbreviation

9

ACROSS

1 ___-up (kind of shot in basketball)
4 What a parent might tell you to clean up
8 "When ___ your age ...": 2 words
12 "How was ___ know?": 2 words
13 Plenty: 2 words
14 Square piece with a letter on it, in the game Scrabble
15 "I need help!"
16 Curved roof on top of some sports stadiums
17 Nasty food given to pigs
18 The last word in a prayer
20 Kind of fruit
22 "You are what you ___"
23 What someone tells you to do when they're taking your picture
25 Imitated a cow
27 Put frosting on a cake
28 Beginning of the alphabet
29 Sirloin or T-bone
31 You sweep with it
33 Relative of a gorilla
34 Common answer to the question, "How are you?"
36 Body parts that blink
38 Not great, just okay: Hyphenated
40 Shredded paper with your hands
42 What people shout to encourage a bullfighter
43 Country in the Middle East
44 Female animals that have wool
45 2000 pounds
46 "Look ___ when I'm talking to you!": 2 words
47 Rests on a bench
48 Stopping place

DOWN

1 One of the Simpsons
2 Tiny particles that all things are made of
3 He chased that "flea-bitten varmint," Bugs Bunny: 2 words
4 Furious
5 Run away and get married
6 More than none, but not all
7 What boiling water turns into

8 "___ a miracle!"
9 He chased the Road Runner: 3 words
10 "That's ___ off my mind!": 2 words
11 Labor Day is in this month: Abbreviation
19 "Have a ___ day!"
21 Sound a lion makes
24 It falls off a tree in autumn
26 Long, skinny musical instrument
29 Football or baseball, for example

30 You fly them in the air on windy days
31 Kind of cap worn by a French person
32 Cantaloupe is this type of fruit
33 Continent that China is in
35 "___ get it!" ("This finally makes sense!"): 2 words
37 Put in the mailbox
39 Number of horns on a unicorn
41 Suffix for "lion" or "count"

ACROSS

1 Number of singers in a duet
4 That lady
7 ___ beam (high-tech device)
12 Electric ___ (kind of fish)
13 A cook fries things in it
14 Opposite of "dead"
15 Mr. Flanders, on "The Simpsons"
16 "Jack ___ Jill went up the hill ..."
17 Measured how long something took to happen
18 Three of a ___ (Yahtzee category)
20 Sound the Road Runner makes
21 Use your brain
23 Salad ___ (where to make your own salad)
24 Room where people do science experiments
27 Sound of a horn
28 "Are we there ___?"
29 List of food in a restaurant
30 It has a shell and a yolk
31 Animal that might be Persian or Siamese
32 Some people write these before shopping for groceries
33 It might be stuck in the top of a bottle
35 Cab
36 Not below
38 Friend of Bashful and Grumpy
39 It can clean up a spill on the floor
42 Times when store prices are lower than usual
43 "Roses ___ red ..."
44 "Humpty Dumpty sat ___ wall": 2 words
45 Person who tries to find jobs for an actor
46 What you say if you agree with someone
47 ___ York City

DOWN

1 Half of twenty
2 ___ Willie Winkie
3 He was a merry old soul: 3 words
4 Hit someone on the bottom
5 It's at the end of the arm
6 Dead-___ street
7 "See you ___, alligator!"

8 Tell ___ (say something that's not true): 2 words

9 He met a pieman going to the fair: 2 words

10 Word that can come after "Christmas"

11 "Scarlet" is this color

19 Invisible ___ (stuff that makes writing you can't see)

20 Animal that hangs upside down in caves

21 Casper, ___ Friendly Ghost

22 Fat pig

23 Gamble

25 Insect that lives in a hill

26 A lot of kids ride it to school

28 Big, hairy mountain animal

29 Scramble

31 Brand of toothpaste

32 Things you use to tie your shoes

34 Microwave ___

35 Ripped

36 Stubborn ___ mule: 2 words

37 Sack

38 April Fools' ___

40 Small number

41 Where a cat's claw is

11

ACROSS

1 Tool that's used to cut wood

4 Health ___ (where some people go to lose weight)

7 Had a part in a movie

12 State where Mobile and Montgomery are: Abbreviation

13 ___ driver (someone who gets paid for driving people around)

14 Not tight

15 Cable network named for Walt: 2 words

18 Animals that lay eggs

19 "How ___ you doing?"

20 A belt goes around this part of the body

22 Where the elbow is

23 Building where people exercise

26 "Money ___ everything!"

27 Pinocchio's nose grew when he told one

28 Bambi was this kind of animal

29 Game with a person called "it"

30 Sticky stuff that's used to make roads

31 Jeans, for example

32 Served a meal to

33 Give someone a job

34 Cable network that shows funny stuff: 2 words

40 "I couldn't get ___ in edgewise!" ("They wouldn't let me talk!"): 2 words

41 Noah's ___

42 On your birthday, this number goes up by one

43 Coin with Abraham Lincoln's face on it

44 Something to play with

45 ___ cabin (wooden house)

DOWN

1 Down in the dumps

2 Prince ___ (who Aladdin pretended to be, in the movie)

3 ___ machine (something to clean your clothes)

4 Odor

5 Spends money

6 The first three letters

7 ___ clock (it wakes you up in the morning)

8 Ice cream holder

9 Really heavy weight

10 Ending for "Japan"

11 State whose capital is Dover: Abbreviation

1	2	3	■	4	5	6	■	7	8	9	10	11
12			■	13			■	14				
15			16				17					
■	■	18				■	19			■	■	■
20	21				■	22			■	23	24	25
26				■	27			■	28			
29			■	30			■	31				
■	■	32			■	33				■	■	■
34	35	36			37				■	38	39	
40				■	41			■	42			
43				■	44			■	45			

16 What a bird builds

17 Animal that looks a lot like a rabbit

20 Sense of humor

21 Big ___ house: 2 words

22 ___ conditioner (cooling device)

23 Person who's in charge of an army

24 "You ain't seen nothing ___!"

25 Abbreviation before a wife's name

27 "___ and the Tramp"

28 It's thrown at a bull's-eye

30 ___ bear (kind of stuffed animal)

31 "___ and the Brain" (cartoon show)

32 Kind of plant whose leaves are called "fronds"

33 Superman or Wonder Woman, for example

34 "Mamma in her kerchief, and I in my ___" (part of a famous Christmas poem)

35 Be in debt

36 Start of the school week: Abbreviation

37 Garfield is one

38 A while ___ (in the past)

39 Lower limb

ACROSS

1 Chair
5 The least important piece in chess
9 "I've ___ an idea!"
12 Fairy ___ (kind of story)
13 Black-and-white brand of cookie
14 King Kong was one
15 Baseball team from Georgia: 2 words
18 A golfer sets a ball on top of it
19 "Oh what fun ___ to ride ..." (line in "Jingle Bells"): 2 words
20 Ernie's friend on "Sesame Street"
21 Ending for "north" or "south"
22 Slippery sea creature
23 Some soft drinks
24 Machine that attaches to a TV: Abbreviation
25 "Crime does not ___"
26 Have the same opinion
29 Automobile
30 Soft hat
33 Grime that's found in a chimney
34 Tiny hole in a person's skin
35 "Much ___ About Nothing" (play by William Shakespeare)
36 Baseball team from Texas: 2 words
39 Suffix that means "most"
40 Got another year older
41 In this place
42 Look at
43 Part of a Mr. Potato Head set
44 Parts of a Mr. Potato Head set

DOWN

1 North Carolina or North Dakota, for example
2 "Peter, Peter, pumpkin ___ ..."
3 Woody ___ (famous movie director)
4 The mad ___ party (scene in "Alice in Wonderland")
5 "Harry ___ and the Goblet of Fire"
6 Thin as ___: 2 words
7 Spiders spin them
8 Neither this ___ that
9 What a judge pounds in the courtroom

10 Soap ___ (TV show that's on in the afternoon)

11 Quizzes

16 Nephew's sister

17 "It's ___!" (what a nurse might tell a new father): 2 words

23 "Who ___?" ("It's not important")

24 Doctors for dogs, for short

25 It includes floats and marching bands

26 What's left after something burns

27 Mother ___ (writer of children's stories)

28 Path that a newspaper deliverer takes

29 They hold scoops of ice cream

30 Mariah ___ (pop singer)

31 Love a lot

32 Gets in place for a photo

34 ___ stick (toy you bounce on)

37 Light brown

38 Off ___ wall (crazy)

13

ACROSS

1 Dinner ___ movie (where some people go on dates): 2 words
5 Come out of a faucet very slowly
9 Male child
12 It helps hold a tree into the ground
13 State that's north of Missouri
14 Female who says "baa"
15 Candy with nuts in it: 2 words
17 Insect that might be eaten by an aardvark
18 Month after April
19 Put into storage
21 Sam-___ (character in "Green Eggs and Ham"): Hyphenated
24 Body part with a nail
26 Word on a triangular street sign
29 Food made from chopped-up cabbage
31 ___ up (totally finish)
33 Princess ___ ("Star Wars" character)
34 Offered a job to
36 Stay ___ (don't go anywhere)
38 Where a lion lives
39 Meat that comes from cows
41 Kanga's child, in "Winnie-the-Pooh"
43 "___ be a monkey's uncle!"
45 Candy with nuts in it: 2 words
50 Little wooden thing on a golf course
51 "Look before you ___"
52 Finished
53 Desperate cry for help
54 Not crazy
55 Observes

DOWN

1 Where your funny bone is
2 Neither here ___ there
3 Animal that barks
4 Part of a molecule
5 "What ___ say?" ("Please repeat that"): 2 words
6 Steal from
7 "As ___ saying ...": 2 words
8 Birthday ___ (celebration)
9 Plant that grows in the ocean
10 Possess
11 It can be used to catch a lot of fish
16 Grain that's sometimes used to feed horses

20 ___ and vinegar (salad toppings)

21 Suffix that means "sort of"

22 "___ Baba and the Forty Thieves"

23 Game played with small round objects

25 Supposedly, the "sixth sense": Abbreviation

27 ___ down (go to bed)

28 ___ Quayle (George Bush's vice president)

30 Tiny

32 Continent where France and Italy are

35 Hands out the cards

37 "It hit me like a ___ of bricks"

40 Insect that might bother a pet

42 Numbers that aren't evens

43 "___ about time!" ("Finally!")

44 Zodiac sign whose symbol is a lion

46 What a boy becomes when he grows up

47 Frank's brother, in the Hardy Boys books

48 Number said right before "liftoff!"

49 "You bet!"

14

ACROSS

1 Conceals
6 They try to sell things
9 Like two peas in a ___ (very similar)
12 Step ___ (move out of the way)
13 Permit
14 "In one ___ and out the other"
15 Where actors in a play are
16 Robert E. ___ (general in the Civil War)
17 Attempt
18 "___ Newt" (cartoon show)
20 Part of a book
22 "Rub-a-dub-dub, three men ___ tub": 2 words
24 Tool for a carpenter
26 Big
29 Toys that go around and around
31 What you give to a good waiter
33 Rotate
34 What you sip a drink through
36 At this time
38 Peanut butter ___ jelly sandwich
39 "What's the big ___?" ("What do you think you're doing?")
41 Opposite of "rich"
43 "Peter ___"
45 "Last one in ___ rotten egg!": 2 words
47 Tools for scraping up leaves
50 "And so on": Abbreviation
51 Get ___ of (remove)
52 The first host of "Blue's Clues"
53 "Golly!"
54 What you might call your father
55 Pitched

DOWN

1 "What ___ four wheels and flies?"
2 Ending for "novel" or "column"
3 Secret identity of Wonder Woman: 2 words
4 Border
5 They're planted in a garden
6 "___ aboard!"

7 Not shallow

8 What robbers do

9 Secret identity of Spider-Man: 2 words

10 It moves a kayak along

11 Lacking moisture

19 Weekend day: Abbreviation

21 ___ station (place to get fuel)

22 "___ no big deal"

23 "Do ___ pass Go ..." (Monopoly instructions)

25 Finish in first place

27 ___ rummy (card game)

28 Dead-___ street

30 Depressed

32 "___ Goes the Weasel"

35 Strange

37 Most terrible

40 Japan is part of this continent

42 What a witness has to take, in the courtroom

43 It helps hold down a tent

44 Consumed

46 Find a sum

48 Cain and Abel's mother

49 Do some stitching

15

ACROSS

1 Speedy
5 Parts of a fancy stereo system
9 Sound made by a woodpecker
12 The state where most Mormons live
13 It keeps a plant in the ground
14 "___ only as directed" (warning on medicine bottles)
15 Nevada city
16 Capital of South Carolina
18 Big brass instrument
20 Put ___ happy face (smile): 2 words
21 A lamb says it
23 Commercials
25 Destroys a balloon
29 Toymaker at the North Pole
30 Signs of sadness
33 Little white ___ (fib)
34 Like one end of a swimming pool
36 Peg used by Tiger Woods
37 "Are we having fun ___?"
38 Letters between Q and U
41 Old MacDonald had one

43 Capital of Hawaii
47 "I'll leave it ___ you" ("It's your decision"): 2 words
50 "You ___ here" (words on a mall map)
51 Dollar bills with George Washington on them
52 Made a knot
53 Moisture that forms on grass
54 You turn it in a book
55 Hour ___ (pointer on a clock)

DOWN

1 Mink coat, for example
2 Gobbled up
3 Capital of New Mexico: 2 words
4 Old-style word for "you"
5 Place with pinball machines and video games
6 Sound from a calf
7 Marco ___ (game played in a swimming pool)
8 Really surprise
9 You take a bath in it
10 "Do ___ say!": 2 words

11 Split ___ soup

17 It might show you how to find a treasure

19 The only mammal that flies

21 Where you sleep

22 Ginger ___ (bubbly drink)

24 "Little Miss Muffet ___ on a tuffet ..."

26 Capital of Washington

27 Chocolate cream ___ (kind of dessert)

28 ___ the table (get ready for dinner)

31 Say no

32 "Under the ___" (song in "The Little Mermaid")

35 Expert

39 It's fed to pigs

40 Fish that's sometimes used for sandwiches

42 Babe ___ (famous baseball player)

43 "I've ___ it up to here!" ("I'm fed up!")

44 Valuable stuff that miners find

45 Original

46 Drumstick

48 Five times two

49 Kind of strange

ACROSS

1 "It ___ bad taste in my mouth": 2 words
6 Fast plane
9 Lily ___
12 Hank ___ (baseball player who hit the most home runs)
13 Tuscaloosa is a city in this state: Abbreviation
14 A man might wear one around his neck
15 She sang "... Baby One More Time": 2 words
18 ___ sauce (condiment at Chinese restaurants)
19 Slippery as an ___
20 ___ constrictor (kind of snake)
23 What the Russian word "da" means in English
25 Intelligent
29 Direction on a compass
31 Gloomy
33 Dog created by the cartoonist Jim Davis
34 Makes a picture of
36 Drink that can be brewed
38 Boy, to his parents
39 "___ little teapot, short and stout ...": 2 words
41 "And many others": Abbreviation
43 She sang "If You Had My Love": 2 words
50 Baltic ___ (space in Monopoly): Abbreviation
51 "___ la la" (sounds in a song)
52 Scent
53 Damp
54 Scalding
55 Put together, as a bookcase: 2 words

DOWN

1 Room where people study chemistry
2 Unit of corn
3 The end of the school week: Abbreviation
4 Little babies
5 Irritate
6 Bird that might be blue
7 "What ___ can I say?"
8 Cassettes
9 Group that might hold an "open house": Abbreviation
10 What's inside a football
11 ___ Moines
16 "You're a sight for sore ___!"
17 Ticklish "Sesame Street" character

20 Word that can go after "bunk" or "flower"

21 It's used to row a boat

22 Happy ___ clam: 2 words

24 It comes after 3-Down: Abbreviation

26 They encourage you to buy things

27 ___ de Janeiro (city in Brazil)

28 The best score you can get in gymnastics

30 Someone whose brother or sister has the same birthday

32 Fawn, when it grows up

35 The most common last name in America

37 Book of maps

40 Big, bushy hairstyle

42 Center of an apple

43 Part of the mouth

44 First woman in the Bible

45 It's on a basketball hoop

46 Snack on

47 You can boil water in it

48 Large Australian bird

49 Laser's sound, sometimes

ACROSS

1 "___ the season to be jolly ..."
4 Word on a light switch
7 Food at an Italian restaurant
12 It's found inside a 28-Across
13 Character in "Winnie-the-Pooh"
14 Felt sore
15 Where you receive letters and magazines
17 Gets wrinkles out of clothes
18 Help out
19 At no cost
20 "It ___ my fault!"
23 What Otto drives, on "The Simpsons"
24 Sheep's sound
27 "That's not ___ idea": 2 words
28 Writing instrument
29 The president before Carter
30 Move quickly
31 Equal score for both teams
32 ___-up (confused)
33 Truth or ___ (game)
35 "It's ___ your own good"

36 Pay-TV
38 Large, portable music system: 2 words
42 Not below
43 "___ Mother Hubbard went to the cupboard ..."
44 "I won't take this ___ longer!"
45 Dallas is in this state
46 Says "all right"
47 "___-Mania" (cartoon about a whirling animal)

DOWN

1 Tiny ___ (character in "A Christmas Carol")
2 Once ___ while: 2 words
3 Enjoy a winter sport
4 The path that a planet takes
5 What you eat
6 Animal that's sometimes hunted by hounds
7 Groups of two
8 Unit of measure that a farmer would use
9 What new loafers are contained in
10 One plus two plus three plus four

11 They interrupt TV shows

16 Solid ground

19 ___ and games

20 The Revolutionary ___

21 The monkey in "Aladdin"

22 Play area where you might build castles

23 Honey maker

25 "___ you serious?"

26 Do some arithmetic

28 Coconut cream ___

29 Not flexible

31 An orchard has them

32 States of mind

34 Thomas Edison's middle name

35 Kind of music that Bob Dylan is famous for

36 Common pet

37 Honest ___ (Lincoln's nickname)

38 What a ghost says

39 A baseball player swings it

40 Like a bump ___ log: 2 words

41 End of the alphabet

ACROSS

1 Touches softly
5 Like a giant
9 Sticky stuff that comes from a tree and is used to make syrup
12 Busy as ___: 2 words
13 Notion
14 What Spanish people shout at a bullfight
15 The ___ Ranger (Tonto's friend)
16 A cat says it
17 U.S. government spy agency: Abbreviation
18 Religious men who take vows of poverty
20 More likable
22 What you might do on the side of a mountain
23 Party thrower
27 Places where lions live
28 Person who watches a sports event
31 Walk back and forth, back and forth
33 Printing mistake, like "teh" instead of "the"
34 Thing on a shark's back
37 All by oneself
39 State that's next to New Hampshire
41 Letters between R and V
42 Sea animal that's used as an ingredient in chowder

46 Most tables have four of them
47 Black stuff used for paving roads
48 The March ___ ("Alice in Wonderland" character)
49 The opening in a piggy bank that you put the coins into
50 Paintings, sculptures, etc.
51 Not shut
52 ___ and ends (various things)

DOWN

1 Coconuts grow on these trees
2 "I can read you like ___!": 2 words
3 Where Andre Agassi plays his sport: 2 words
4 Hide and ___
5 ___ Allen (actor who was on "Home Improvement")
6 It can come after "Gator" or "lemon"
7 Sign of the zodiac whose symbol is a lion
8 Grassy area that has to be mowed
9 Where Mia Hamm plays her sport: 2 words

10 Someone from another planet

11 Certain fruits

19 "___ sells seashells by the seashore" (tongue twister)

21 "What did ___ wrong?": 2 words

24 The month that Halloween is in: Abbreviation

25 Another word for 29-Down

26 Gently touch someone on the shoulder

29 Place where a pig lives

30 Name of "the piper's son" in a nursery rhyme

31 Spaghetti and macaroni are this kind of food

32 Place in a church where people get married

35 "___ we trust" (phrase on all U.S. money): 2 words

36 Robins' homes

38 A sound that you hear again after you say it

40 Too

43 You form one when you sit down

44 "What ___ you talking about?"

45 Guys

19

ACROSS

1 Someone who looks down on other people
5 Money
9 ___-Man (video game character who eats dots)
12 The daughter of Hägar the Horrible, in comics
13 ___ code (the first part of a phone number)
14 The last word in the Pledge of Allegiance
15 "Look ___ from my point of view": 2 words
16 Building where grain is made into flour
17 ___ Grande (famous river)
18 Tony the Tiger's cereal: 2 words
21 The first two-digit number
22 Portland is a city in this state: Abbreviation
23 Hair on a horse's neck
24 Black-eyed ___ (little vegetable)
25 Pig farmer's enclosure
27 Plus
30 Homophone of "eight"
31 "Who Wants to ___ Millionaire": 2 words
34 Cereal with a honey taste: 2 words

38 "What do I ___ you?" ("How much money do I have to pay?")
39 He was Clinton's vice president
40 What poison ivy might make you do
41 Father of Rod and Todd Flanders, on "The Simpsons"
42 "Halt! Who ___ there?" (what a guard might say)
43 "My country, 'tis of ___ ..."
44 100 of them make a century: Abbreviation
45 What you get when you ask for change for a five-dollar bill
46 Looks at

DOWN

1 The long, thin part of an arrow
2 "The Hunchback of ___ Dame"
3 Vegetable that makes people cry when they peel it
4 Kibbles 'n' ___ (brand of dog food)
5 What a photographer uses

6 Go for ___ (travel by car): 2 words
7 ___-centered (vain)
8 One of the rooms in the board game Clue
9 Jacket that has a hood
10 Martian, for example
11 "___ but no cigar!"
19 Tic-tac-___
20 Girl in "Little Women"
24 What the vegetable at 24-Across comes in
25 What you feel when there's a lot of pressure on you
26 Drink that's made from leaves

27 Extreme suffering
28 Further down
29 Vehicles that are pulled by dogs in some races
30 Have the same opinion as someone else
31 Clean oneself
32 The person who introduces other speakers at an assembly
33 What's left after something is burned
35 "Leggo my ___!" (frozen waffles' ad slogan)
36 Time for lunch
37 What baseball batters try to get

20

ACROSS

1 "Well, ___ be darned!"
4 ___ Diego, California
7 ___ hygiene (brushing one's teeth)
11 "Have a ___" ("Use this chair")
13 Prefix that means "the environment"
14 ___ stick (bouncy toy)
15 Harry Potter's school
17 Wives of rams
18 Homophone for "oh"
19 High social rank in England
21 "Do you know who ___?": 2 words
24 An exterminator might kill it
26 Your fingers and toes have them
29 Disease that people often get in the winter
30 24-___ gold
32 "That's ___ funny!"
33 People put chemicals in their swimming pools and aquariums to help get rid of this
35 ___ Wednesday (time before Easter)
36 Wise ___ (smart aleck)
37 Sudden burst of wind
39 British people drink a lot of it
41 Freezing
43 She's one of Harry Potter's best friends
48 "You're the only ___ can trust": 2 words
49 In the past
50 Gives a massage
51 El ___, Texas
52 1, 2, and 3, for example: Abbreviation
53 The sound a woodpecker makes on a tree

DOWN

1 Suffix that means "kind of"
2 Sign of the zodiac
3 Jet ___ (what people get when they fly from one time zone to another)
4 One of the tennis-playing Williams sisters
5 Be in a play
6 Where your nostrils are
7 "Carmen" is a famous one
8 Last name of Harry Potter's author
9 Middle ___ (when people aren't young or old)
10 ___ Angeles

44

12 Number of people in a duo

16 Stops sleeping

20 "The Star-Spangled Banner" is the national ___

21 "___ tree falls in the forest, does it make a sound?": 2 words

22 100%

23 What Harry Potter calls non-magical people

25 "___ la la" (sounds in a song refrain)

27 "Skip to My ___"

28 Where a boar and sow might be

31 Houston's baseball team

34 Word that sometimes goes before "visual"

38 "Better late ___ never"

40 ___ conditioning

41 Short word for a police officer

42 Put ___ happy face (smile): 2 words

44 A conceited person has a big one

45 ___ of this world (really great)

46 Shaquille O'Neal plays in this group: Abbreviation

47 Supposed ability to read minds: Abbreviation

ACROSS

1 Movie about a pig that wants to be a sheepdog
5 What old fruit will do
8 One ___ time (not all together): 2 words
11 Puts grease on
12 Phrase that's said during a wedding: 2 words
13 Was in front of followers
14 Drink containers that can be recycled: 2 words
17 Black animal that you might see on Halloween
18 Last name of the person who wrote "Curious George"
19 Proud ___ peacock: 2 words
22 "So near and ___ so far"
24 Arguments that aren't very serious
28 ___-door neighbor (person who lives very close to you)
30 Hand of a hound
32 What you could hear if you shouted in a cave
33 Nerdy person
35 Word that can come after "note" or "lily"
37 Normal number of toes

38 Boat that carried all the animals, in the Bible
40 The color of a cherry
42 Drink containers that can be recycled: 2 words
48 Moved really fast
49 ___ and don'ts
50 Joint in your leg
51 The first even number
52 Ram's wife
53 ___ good example (what role models do): 2 words

DOWN

1 Marshy place where cranberries grow
2 Feel unhealthy
3 Tell a secret
4 What a teacher might ask you to write
5 Bone in your chest
6 Smell
7 Carries around
8 "___ men are created equal"
9 Wooden peg used in golf
10 Want ___ (what some people read when they're trying to find jobs)

15 Part of a staircase

16 Use a keyboard

19 Tom ___ Jerry (cartoon pair)

20 Homophone for "so"

21 Tool that can cut down a tree

23 ___ water (what comes out of a kitchen faucet)

25 Put on an ___ (pretend)

26 Jack-in-___-box

27 Child who's a boy

29 Group of athletes

31 Like June weather, usually

34 She marries the groom

36 Packs of playing cards

39 ___-it-all (smart aleck)

41 Great ___ (kind of dog)

42 What museums contain

43 Break the ___ (do something illegal)

44 Card game with "REVERSE" and "DRAW 4" cards

45 Make ___ of (find something to do with)

46 What a volleyball gets hit over

47 Caribbean ___ (big body of water)

22

ACROSS

1 Shut a door noisily
5 ___ and forth
9 Sounds that come after "tra" in a song: 2 words
10 Have a sore muscle
11 What candles are made of
14 Take ___ (sleep for a little while): 2 words
15 Lima ___ (kind of vegetable)
16 Butter ___ (flavor of Life Savers)
17 Revolutions ___ minute (what RPM stands for, on a record)
18 Opposite of "west"
19 Nick at ___ (what Nickelodeon calls its evening programs)
20 Spread messily, as finger paints
22 Summer is one
24 Music sometimes comes on them: Abbreviation
25 Fire ___ (insect that stings)
26 Places where you go bowling
29 Makes a sketch
31 Animal that roars

32 Bumper ___ (amusement park vehicles)
34 ___ up (misbehave)
36 "Monsters, ___" (animated movie)
37 You might skip it on a playground
38 "Twinkle, Twinkle, Little ___"
39 What some people say if they see a mouse
40 A flower, or a part of the eye
41 Measure of land
42 Things that you toss the rings over when you're playing ringtoss
43 "This is fun!"

DOWN

1 Smack in the face
2 A highway sometimes has four of them
3 Timer that wakes people up: 2 words
4 You might use one in a treasure hunt
5 Elephant whose wife's name is Celeste
6 Good cards to have in poker

```
┌──┬──┬──┬──┬──┬──┬──┬──┬──┬──┬──┬──┬──┐
│1 │2 │3 │4 │██│5 │6 │7 │8 │██│██│██│██│
├──┼──┼──┼──┼──┼──┼──┼──┼──┼──┼──┼──┼──┤
│9 │  │  │  │██│10│  │  │  │██│11│12│13│
├──┼──┼──┼──┼──┼──┼──┼──┼──┼──┼──┼──┼──┤
│14│  │  │  │██│15│  │  │  │██│16│  │  │
├──┼──┼──┼──┼──┼──┼──┼──┼──┼──┼──┼──┼──┤
│17│  │  │██│18│  │  │  │██│19│  │  │  │
├──┼──┼──┼──┼──┼──┼──┼──┼──┼──┼──┼──┼──┤
│██│20│  │21│  │  │██│22│23│  │  │  │  │
├──┼──┼──┼──┼──┼──┼──┼──┼──┼──┼──┼──┼──┤
│██│██│24│  │  │██│██│25│  │  │██│██│██│
├──┼──┼──┼──┼──┼──┼──┼──┼──┼──┼──┼──┼──┤
│26│27│  │  │██│28│  │29│  │  │  │30│██│
├──┼──┼──┼──┼──┼──┼──┼──┼──┼──┼──┼──┼──┤
│31│  │  │  │██│32│33│  │  │██│34│  │35│
├──┼──┼──┼──┼──┼──┼──┼──┼──┼──┼──┼──┼──┤
│36│  │  │██│37│  │  │  │██│38│  │  │  │
├──┼──┼──┼──┼──┼──┼──┼──┼──┼──┼──┼──┼──┤
│39│  │  │██│40│  │  │  │██│41│  │  │  │
├──┼──┼──┼──┼──┼──┼──┼──┼──┼──┼──┼──┼──┤
│██│██│██│██│42│  │  │  │██│43│  │  │  │
└──┴──┴──┴──┴──┴──┴──┴──┴──┴──┴──┴──┴──┘
```

7 Has a conversation

8 Boyfriend of Barbie

11 Timer that's worn on the arm

12 It might go before "biography" or "mobile"

13 Comic-book group that includes Wolverine and Cyclops: Hyphenated

18 Not difficult

19 The dog in "Peter Pan"

21 Where Adam and Eve lived

23 A basset hound has long ones

26 "I cannot tell ___" (what young George Washington said): 2 words

27 Finish ___ (where runners end a race)

28 The number of points each team has

29 Gown

30 Frighten

33 Eat like ___ (wolf your food down): 2 words

35 Thing you'd find in a forest

37 Tear

38 Tool used by carpenters

ACROSS

1 "The ___ is clear" ("I don't see any danger")
6 What performers do
9 Not bright
12 "___ in the court!" (something a judge says)
13 Younger version of 11-Down
14 "Birds ___ feather flock together": 2 words
15 How fast a musician plays the music
16 Military rank
18 "Leave ___ to me": 2 words
20 Drink that contains caffeine
21 Distant
23 Color of a camel
25 Number
29 Country that's next to Iraq
31 Not high
33 Jay ___ (host of "The Tonight Show")
34 Opposite of "above"
36 Beavers might build one in a river
38 Snooze
39 It would catch a tightrope walker who fell, in the circus
41 A "soapbox derby" is this kind of event

43 Military rank
47 Relating to life out in the country
50 "___ thing leads to another"
51 Touch gently, as with a washcloth
52 Like really old bread
53 What a happy dog's tail will do
54 There are ten of these in a decade: Abbreviation
55 "Hi!"

DOWN

1 You might put on a sleeping bag on it
2 State that's south of Washington: Abbreviation
3 Military rank
4 Autumn begins in this month: Abbreviation
5 Kind of fish that might be "speckled" or "rainbow"
6 As easy as ___
7 Jacket
8 Used a keyboard to write something
9 ___ favor (help someone out): 2 words

10 "Not ___ can help it!": 2 words
11 Guy
17 A peacock has a fancy one
19 Buddy
21 Little white lie
22 "A fool and his money ___ soon parted"
24 Show agreement by moving your head
26 Military rank
27 "... and pretty maids all ___ row": 2 words
28 Toy that spins around
30 You're not supposed to do it: Hyphenated

32 The Civil ___
35 Girl in "Peter Pan"
37 Swamp
40 Drop that comes from the eye
42 ___ as a button
43 Animal that has calves
44 "Little Miss Muffet sat ___ tuffet ...": 2 words
45 The shin is part of it
46 A ton weighs 2000 of these: Abbreviation
48 ___ of a sudden (with no warning)
49 One of the 12 signs of the zodiac

ACROSS

1 Machine you could find outside a bank: Abbreviation

4 "___ little piggy went to market ..."

8 Poison ivy might give you one

12 Sound heard on Halloween

13 Stop

14 The largest continent

15 Something you might take to the beach

17 Wacky

18 Olive ___ (Popeye's girlfriend)

19 "What can ___ to help?": 2 words

21 Part of a cat's paw

24 Something you might take to the beach

28 Fuel that's sometimes called "black gold"

29 Break into a million pieces

31 Ending for "meteor"

32 Something you might take to the beach

34 Less than twice

35 "___ for 'apple'": 2 words

36 Took a look at

38 Thing

41 Something you might take to the beach

46 Rescue

47 Very long classic story

48 "Postage ___" (marking on some envelopes)

49 Tools used by lumberjacks

50 Sticky substances that come out of trees

51 Comfortable room in the house

DOWN

1 Aladdin's pet monkey, in the movie

2 "The piper's son," in the nursery rhyme

3 Large group of people

4 Those people

5 Long, thin area between rooms

6 Chicago's state: Abbreviation

7 What detergents try to get out of clothes

8 It's used for shaving

9 Hungry ___ bear: 2 words

10 What preachers might talk about in their sermons

11 Horses eat it

16 Make a boat move

20 Play-___ (material similar to clay)
21 Corn on the ___
22 ___ Kim (rap singer)
23 State next to Mississippi: Abbreviation
24 Got into a chair
25 Relatives
26 "And so on, and so on": Abbreviation
27 Bruce ___ (star of martial arts movies)
29 Water-___ (have fun on a lake)
30 Untidy places
33 Jan, Dan, and Fran, for example

34 Bird that hoots
36 Cut just a little
37 "Now I know my ___ ..." (line in the alphabet song)
38 "This ___ test of the Emergency Broadcast System": 2 words
39 Sales ___ (extra amount you pay for something)
40 Wife of Adam
42 Put ___ fight: 2 words
43 A little weird
44 ___ ball (the white ball on a pool table)
45 Famous male doll

25

ACROSS

1 "Do not ___ Go, do not collect $200"

5 The deepest kind of male voice

9 "As I was going to St. Ives, I ___ a man with seven wives"

12 "Don't have ___, man!": 2 words

13 Stumble

14 Poison ___ (plant that makes you itch)

15 Card game for one person

17 Part of the mouth

18 "___ Kangaroo Down, Sport" (song): 2 words

19 Waltz or tango, for example

21 Opposite of "question": Abbreviation

22 ___ Lane (Superman's girlfriend)

26 Fishermen sometimes use them

27 Card game where you don't want to end up with a particular card: 2 words

29 Rock back and forth

32 Week divisions

33 ___ Snorkel (character in "Beetle Bailey"): Abbreviation

36 Buckets

38 More original

40 Kind of tree

41 Card game also known as "blackjack": Hyphenated

45 It comes after "lemon" and "orange" in names of drinks

46 "That's terrible!": 2 words

47 One of the Great Lakes

48 ___ and reel (things used in fishing)

49 Peas come in them

50 Has a view of

DOWN

1 Noodles are this kind of food

2 Flip ___ (use luck to decide): 2 words

3 Bottom parts of shoes

4 Move in a pool

5 Group that includes Cub Scouts and Webelos: Abbreviation

6 ___ Baba

7 What Marcie calls Peppermint Patty

8 Drove faster than 55 miles per hour

9 A.A. ___ (author of "Winnie-the-Pooh")

10 Kick out of an apartment

11 A, B, AB, and O are the four main blood ___

16 William ___ (archer who shot an apple off his son's head)

20 "Come ___ get it!"

23 Off-the-wall

24 "___ Yankee Doodle Dandy": 2 words

25 "What did you ___?" ("I couldn't hear you")

27 Olive ___ (character in cartoons)

28 What "ain't" should be in the sentence, "He ain't right"

29 Long, pointy weapon

30 "Where's ___?" (book where you try to find a person in crowded drawings)

31 Pointed a camera

33 Said a cussword

34 Magical being who might grant you three wishes

35 Maple, oak, and apple, for example

37 What a red light means

39 They have brows and lashes

42 "Horton Hears a ___!" (Dr. Seuss book)

43 Conclusion

44 They aren't yeses

26

ACROSS

1 Sit still for a painter
5 Cube of hay
9 What a kitten becomes
12 "That's one small step for ___ ..." (what Neil Armstrong said when he landed on the moon): 2 words
13 Puts frosting on a cake
14 Lincoln's nickname
15 Fruit that's kind of like an orange
17 "Who Wants to ___ Millionaire": 2 words
18 Word that begins a lot of titles
19 Solves "2 + 2," for example
20 Sea animal with a shell
21 Grassy areas around houses
23 They have things for people to buy
25 "___ the fields we go ..." (line in "Jingle Bells")
27 "Do you ___ what I mean?"
28 Frying pan
32 Raise ___ (complain): 2 words
36 Ice cream ___
37 A telephone might have one on its end

39 Good friend
40 Sprinted
41 Fruit that grows in Hawaii
43 Ginger ___ (fizzy drink)
44 Bigger relatives of monkeys
45 ___ off (annoyed)
46 How many shots it's supposed to take, in golf
47 What W means, on a compass
48 They come down from your shoulders

DOWN

1 Peppermint ___ ("Peanuts" character who calls Charlie Brown "Chuck")
2 Big city in Nebraska
3 More sensible
4 London's country: Abbreviation
5 Sparrow or swallow, for example
6 Chemicals that can eat into metal
7 Contact ___ (what some people wear instead of glasses)
8 Ending for "Vietnam"
9 Big, thick wire

	1	2	3	4		5	6	7	8		9	10	11
12						13					14		
15				16							17		
18					19					20			
21			22				23	24					
		25		26		27						
28	29	30			31		32		33	34	35
36				37	38			39			
40			41				42				
43			44				45				
46			47				48				

10 "Fuzzy Wuzzy was ___ ...": 2 words

11 Sports groups

16 Wooden stand used by a painter

20 Treble ___ (symbol on a musical staff)

22 Bob ___ (Republican senator who ran for president against Bill Clinton)

24 "You can ___ horse to water but you can't make him drink": 2 words

26 It tells you how to make a certain food

28 ___ paper (paper that's not needed for anything)

29 ___ bear (cute animal from Australia)

30 Not outer

31 Dial ___ (sounds heard on telephones)

33 Opposite of "lower"

34 Capital of Oregon

35 Toboggans

38 Take a nap

41 What a dog raises if you teach it to "shake hands"

42 School organization: Abbreviation

27

ACROSS

1 Certain piece of chicken
4 A superhero might wear one
8 "___ first you don't succeed, try, try again": 2 words
12 What a person in a rowboat sometimes holds
13 Needs to pay back
14 It's thrown at weddings
15 People press down on them to connect papers together
17 ___ code
18 Part of a hockey goal
19 Measures of intelligence: Abbreviation
20 "... ___ partridge in a pear tree": 2 words
22 When the sun comes up
25 "If it's not ___ much trouble ..."
28 Jump on one foot
29 North ___ (country in Asia)
30 "I'll see what I ___ do"
31 One thing ___ time: 2 words
32 Decorated a cupcake
33 ___ bag (large bag for carrying things around)
34 Stimpy's friend, in cartoons
36 "Happy Birthday to ___"
37 Do what you're told to do
39 Lets loose
44 The ___ Star State (nickname for Texas)
45 Opposite of "good"
46 "___ little teapot ...": 2 words
47 Connect the ___ (simple puzzle)
48 "The Farmer in the ___"
49 Religious woman

DOWN

1 ___ Angeles
2 Swallow up
3 Certain relative
4 Baby horse
5 In ___ of (impressed by)
6 Pay-___-view (kind of TV show)
7 Ending for "lion"
8 Country whose capital is Baghdad
9 Certain relative: 2 words
10 The highest card
11 Popular drink in England

16 It bothered the princess in a famous story

19 ___ good mood (happy): 2 words

20 "I get it!"

21 "That's ___ my problem"

22 "Snow White and the Seven Dwarfs" character

23 "___ we there yet?"

24 The middle of the school week: Abbreviation

26 Grain that might come before "meal"

27 Low number

29 People who are related to you

33 Burnt ___ crisp: 2 words

35 What the holes in needles are called

36 Scream

37 ___ as the hills

38 Ghostly sound

39 The color of beets

40 Christmas ___

41 "___ Abner" (old comic strip)

42 Australian bird that can't fly

43 ___ Antonio, Texas

28

ACROSS

1 "Help!"
4 What comes out of a faucet
9 Bone at the bottom of the face
12 ___ Whitney (inventor of the cotton gin)
13 With no help from anyone else
14 What a glacier is made of
15 Electric fish
16 What a plane does at the end of the flight
17 Butterfly catcher
18 Ending for "differ"
20 Price ___
22 Part of a skeleton
24 Referees blow them
29 Certain insects
30 Kool-___ (fruity drink)
31 Brand of toy that you build things with
32 They fix teeth
34 "It's ___!" (what a doctor might say after a birth): 2 words
35 Ending for "guitar" or "novel"
36 "___ the Force, Luke" (what Obi-Wan told Luke Skywalker in "Star Wars")
37 Lightning ___ (insect that glows)
39 Fixes an article before it goes into a magazine
43 "___ me make this perfectly clear ..."
46 It might be found at the bottom of a fireplace
47 Goes from one place to another
48 Zodiac sign that comes before Virgo
49 It looks like a big mouse
50 Guide a car in the right direction
51 Where clouds and stars are

DOWN

1 Use your eyes
2 Cheer in Mexico
3 Christmas song where "all is calm, all is bright": 2 words
4 ___ Disney
5 Pie ___ mode: 2 words
6 Really heavy weight
7 Beginning's opposite
8 Takes a break
9 Christmas song where "bells on bobtails ring": 2 words

10 Good card to have in the game War

11 Soaking ___

19 Birds build them

21 Book that's filled with maps

22 Not good

23 Number of wheels on a unicycle

24 The past tense of "is"

25 What a baseball batter tries to get

26 Cards that show who you are: Abbreviation

27 A self-important person has a big one

28 Sauce used in Chinese restaurants

33 Things

36 Russia used to be part of it: Abbreviation

37 Candy ___

38 Country in North America: Abbreviation

40 Part of a lowercase "i"

41 "Now ___ seen everything!"

42 A golf ball sits on one before it's hit

44 Frightened sound

45 Something to play with

29

ACROSS

1 A modest person has a small one
4 Moved on a slippery surface
8 Clothing worn when it's cold
12 Cindy-___ Who (little girl in "How the Grinch Stole Christmas")
13 Mexican food
14 ___ browns (chopped-up breakfast food)
15 Crispy treat at a Chinese restaurant: 2 words
18 ___ of a kind (unique)
19 Noisy kind of dance
20 "What are you talking ___?"
23 "A penny ___ your thoughts"
24 Spend
27 Tasting like a lemon
28 ___ Majesty (how people refer to a queen)
29 Smart
30 "The Cat in the ___"
31 Long bench in a church
32 Places for skating
33 Body of water
34 ___ Moines, Iowa
35 Crispy treat that might be shaped like a lion or giraffe: 2 words

42 The dog in "The Wizard of Oz"
43 Animal in "The Wind in the Willows"
44 Plant that can grow along walls
45 Sick as ___: 2 words
46 Big pigs
47 Wooden item used in golf

DOWN

1 Assistant at the North Pole
2 Sticky stuff
3 "Days of ___ Lives" (soap opera)
4 Dangerous thing done on a movie set
5 Division of a highway
6 Water cubes
7 Someone who helps people get well
8 Pork ___
9 Tree that has acorns
10 "___ was saying ...": 2 words
11 All ___ time (constantly)
16 Trip where you walk around and look at the sights

17 Rowing need
20 ___ Wednesday (first day of Lent)
21 ___ constrictor (dangerous snake)
22 "Get ___ of here!" ("Beat it!")
23 ___ and far between (rare)
24 ___ the tail on the donkey (party game)
25 "Don't ___ me!" ("I don't know!")
26 Word of agreement
28 Wellness
29 Its capital is Madison: Abbreviation

31 Vegetable that sounds like a letter of the alphabet
32 Enjoys a book
33 Dirty air in a city
34 Pull something behind you
35 One ___ time: 2 words
36 ___ off (start to fall asleep)
37 "How was ___ know?": 2 words
38 Sound a pigeon makes
39 What a model car comes in before it's built
40 New Year's ___
41 Dark-colored bread

63

30

ACROSS

1 "What will ___ now?":
2 words
4 Flat ___ pancake:
2 words
7 "How long ___ this been going on?"
10 "It hit me like a ___ of bricks"
11 Good-___-nothing (worthless)
12 Wind up a rope
13 Character in "Toy Story":
2 words
16 "Give ___ shot":
2 words
17 Little brat
18 Just for the fun ___:
2 words
21 Had breakfast
22 "In ___ we trust" (phrase on U.S. money)
25 Character in "Toy Story":
2 words
29 Dublin is in this country:
Abbreviation
30 Ending for "Siam"
31 Deer that have large antlers
32 "What ___ supposed to do?": 2 words
33 Out ___ limb: 2 words
35 Character in "Toy Story":
3 words
41 Rub ___ (gloat): 2 words

42 Cousin ___ (hairy character in "The Addams Family")
43 Baboon's relative
44 "Monkey ___, monkey do"
45 Larry, ___, and Curly (the Three Stooges)
46 In the long ___ (over a long period of time)

DOWN

1 "___ the Great Pumpkin, Charlie Brown"
2 What Homer Simpson says when he's upset
3 Half of two
4 Throw ___ (have a temper tantrum): 2 words
5 Piece of furniture that might be in the living room
6 What Little Orphan Annie's dog said
7 Basketball players aim for it
8 Lend a hand
9 ___ as a fox (sneaky)
12 One of Santa's reindeer
14 Brand of crackers
15 Go ___ the flow
18 ___-Wan Kenobi ("Star Wars" person)

19 Mink coat, for example
20 Ending for "critic" or "capital"
21 It changes on your birthday
22 Stuff that makes hair stiffer
23 Big tree
24 They heal the sick: Abbreviation
26 Yellow fruit
27 "What time ___?": 2 words
28 Opposite of "nope"
32 "Four-and-twenty blackbirds baked in ___": 2 words

33 Boy's name that reads the same forward and backward
34 Short letter
35 Beginning for "behave" or "spell"
36 Path followed by a mail carrier: Abbreviation
37 Point a camera
38 Where someone would put a hearing aid
39 Kwik-E-Mart worker on "The Simpsons"
40 Room where there might be a TV

31

ACROSS

1 Farmers plant them
6 Mind-reading ability that some people believe in: Abbreviation
9 Break the ___ (do something illegal)
12 Expect
13 ___ standstill (not moving): 2 words
14 Number that appears on a penny
15 "Here comes ___ Cottontail ..."
16 Eminem's music
17 "See you later!"
18 What water comes out of, in a sink
20 Old cloths
22 ___-Cone (frosty treat)
25 Something a dog says
27 "___ boy!" (delivery room exclamation): 2 words
30 Food you can order in a Mexican restaurant
32 What a baseball player gets credit for when he causes another player to score: Abbreviation
33 Dudley Do-Right was in love with her
34 "I've had it ___ here!": 2 words

35 The Leaning Tower of ___
37 Kind of bread
38 Cincinnati is in this state
40 ___ the nail on the head (be exactly right)
42 "Alley ___" (old comic strip)
44 ___ Van Winkle
46 Trades
50 Winter disease, sometimes
51 Cool ___ cucumber: 2 words
52 Speed ___ (what drivers are supposed to obey)
53 TV commercials
54 ___ Hampshire
55 Doors that you leave through

DOWN

1 Sticky stuff in trees
2 Female sheep
3 Have brunch
4 Try to lose weight
5 Stuff inside a scarecrow
6 ___ of corn
7 Sea creature with five arms
8 One of the Three Bears
9 Sea creature with a hard shell and claws

10 "Are there ___ questions?"

11 Very small

19 Sea creature similar to a dolphin

21 ___ rummy

22 Letters after R

23 Short sleep

24 Sea creature with eight tentacles

26 ___-Wan Kenobi (character in the movie "Star Wars")

28 Sneaky

29 Ginger ___

31 ___ and aah (impressed sounds)

36 What a bride walks down, in church

39 Country that used to have a ruler called a shah

41 Crispy chocolate-covered candy bar

42 Too much ___ good thing: 2 words

43 "___ MacDonald had a farm ..."

45 Kitten's hand

47 "What ___ doing here?": 2 words

48 The stone in the middle of a peach

49 People drive on them: Abbreviation

32

ACROSS

1 Tic-___-toe
4 Square or circle, for example
9 Expert
12 A long time ___
13 Sat down so that an artist could draw you
14 The color of Rudolph's nose
15 Something to write with
16 Really surprise
17 Go off the deep ___ (go crazy)
18 Tarzan's wife
20 Sleep for an hour or so
22 ___ McCartney (one of the Beatles)
24 Tear
27 Polka ___ (circles on clothing)
30 "Well, ___ that special!"
31 Alien spacecraft: Abbreviation
32 Afghanistan is on this continent
33 Heading on Santa's list opposite "naughty"
34 Puppy's bite
35 Place where ideas come from
36 "___ it, you'll like it!"
38 Price
40 Beginning for "cycle" or "angle"

42 Attach to the end: 2 words
45 Sam-___ (Dr. Seuss character): Hyphenated
48 "The Mystery Files of Shelby ___" (former kids' show on Nickelodeon)
49 Mary Tyler ___ (famous actress)
50 State that borders the Pacific Ocean: Abbreviation
51 "Mind your ___ business!"
52 Reads through
53 An animal could be trapped in one

DOWN

1 Kind of dancing
2 In this day and ___ (nowadays)
3 "And" is this part of speech
4 Attention ___ (how long you can pay attention)
5 A baseball player might hit one: 2 words
6 White ___ ghost: 2 words
7 Brand of candy that has its own dispenser
8 The Garden of ___ (place in the Bible)

9 "Before" is this part of speech
10 Stimpy's pal, in cartoons
11 Not even
19 Make a change to an item of clothing
21 The president after Washington
22 What you try to do to your opponent, in wrestling
23 "Just ___ thought!": 2 words
25 "___ Were King of the Forest" (song in "The Wizard of Oz"): 2 words

26 Snack at the movies
28 Kind of metal
29 Dejected
37 Vegetables you might have at Thanksgiving
39 Some dollar bills
40 Number of things in a pair
41 "... and pretty maids all in a ___"
43 Friend of Grumpy and Happy
44 ___ good deed: 2 words
46 "We ___ the World" (song from the 1980s)
47 New York baseball team member

33

ACROSS

1 Tardy
5 Gave a meal to
8 Munched on
11 Some Apple computers
13 First name that can be for either a boy or a girl
14 At this moment
15 Thomas Edison invented it: 2 words
17 It's used to color Easter eggs
18 "___ the ramparts we watched ..." (line in "The Star-Spangled Banner")
19 It shines in the night sky
21 What painters make
24 Will Smith's music
26 In the near future
29 Elias Howe invented it: 2 words
33 What the Earth spins on
34 ___ Lancelot (famous knight)
35 "See-saw, Margery ___" (nursery rhyme)
36 Something a beauty pageant contestant wears
39 Straight line
41 Head covering
43 Alexander Graham Bell invented it
48 Cold cubes
49 "You ___ the weakest link! Good-bye!" (game show phrase)
50 Area in the head that can be affected by hay fever
51 "55 miles ___ hour" (common speed limit)
52 Wager
53 Household animals

DOWN

1 Phil's twin, on "Rugrats"
2 "Where ___?" (lost person's question): 2 words
3 Game in which you shout "Not it!"
4 Sound in a canyon
5 Sickness that sometimes lasts for a week or two
6 Slippery, skinny fish
7 In ___ (owing money)
8 Machine that looks and acts like a human
9 Slinky or Frisbee, for example
10 Female animal on a farm
12 Strict

16 Boast

20 Stuff in a fireplace after a fire

21 Cute ___ button: 2 words

22 Tyrannosaurus ___ (kind of dinosaur)

23 Game that "ties you up in knots"

25 Evenings: Abbreviation

27 "I'm ___ roll!" ("Everything is going just right!"): 2 words

28 ___ and improved

30 "This ___ stickup!" (robber's cry): 2 words

31 Ending for "million"

32 What farmers harvest

37 Take a ___ at it (try something)

38 What you say when the teacher takes attendance

40 A lion tamer holds one

41 Really cool

42 High card

44 ___ down (disappoint)

45 What the Roman numeral I is equal to

46 Cashew, for example

47 Ending for "host"

34

ACROSS

1 Opposite of "more"
5 Pleads
9 What a movie director yells to end a scene
12 In ___ (stuck doing the same thing over and over): 2 words
13 Black-and-white cookie
14 "It's just ___ thought!": 2 words
15 Couple
16 What knees do
17 People sign contracts with them
19 Male deer
21 Spies' group: Abbreviation
22 Shoe with wheels or a blade on the bottom
24 Puts down on paper
26 The calm center of a hurricane
27 People say it as they're getting married: 2 words
28 Dictator
31 The back of a boat
33 Kind of rodent
34 What food that's been in the freezer has to do before you can cook it

36 Mongolia is part of this continent
38 Sailor's greeting
40 Many: 2 words
42 Liverpool's country: Abbreviation
43 Toy that goes up and down on a string: Hyphenated
44 Spare ___ (item in a car's trunk)
45 Piece of golf equipment
46 Just okay, not great: Hyphenated
47 "Children should be ___ and not heard"

DOWN

1 One trip around the track
2 Get rid of pencil marks
3 Three-piece ___ (formal outfit for a man)
4 Tube you can drink through
5 ___ for apples (play a Halloween activity)
6 Kids build things with it: 2 words
7 Robin Williams played one in "Aladdin"

8 Soft drinks

9 A dunce might have one on his head

10 Does something with

11 Kids build things with them

18 "Don't ___ word" ("Be quiet"): 2 words

20 Sand particles

23 What a camper sleeps in

25 "I have no ___" ("Beats me!")

28 They hold your plates, in a cafeteria

29 "Whee!"

30 "___ all, folks!"

31 Said cusswords

32 Three times three

35 Tell ___ (be dishonest): 2 words

37 The Stone ___ (time period when the Flintstones supposedly lived)

39 "___-hoo!" (what you say to get someone's attention)

41 Number of cents in a dime

35

ACROSS

1 Be the champion
4 Zeus was one for the ancient Greeks
7 Applaud
11 Good card in the game twenty-one
12 "Prince ___" (song in "Aladdin")
13 Opposite of "early"
14 Music lover's purchase: 2 words
17 Young person
18 Tool for cutting wood
19 Average score, in golf
22 Was in front of the crowd
24 Has on
28 Great Lake that forms part of Pennsylvania's border
30 Word that goes with "neither"
32 Faucet problem
33 Black-and-white animal
35 Valuable stone
37 "___ Story" (animated movie)
38 Country that got its independence in 1776: Abbreviation
40 Homophone of "dough"
42 Music lover's purchase: 2 words

48 "Step ___!" ("Hurry!"): 2 words
49 Gardening tool
50 Lemon meringue ___ (kind of dessert)
51 People sleep in them
52 Organ you hear with
53 ___ Turner (famous slave)

DOWN

1 Card game for two people
2 It comes with a cup of soda
3 Where a man has his Adam's apple
4 Place to grow vegetables or flowers
5 "This ___ man, he played one ..."
6 Quick swims
7 Scratched like a cat
8 Put down
9 Wolfed down
10 Miles ___ gallon
15 Kind of fuel
16 The ___ of gravity (scientific rule)
19 ___ dispenser (certain candy container)

20 "You ___ what you eat"
21 Prime ___ (kind of beef)
23 Dalmatian or dachshund, for example
25 State-of-the-___ (high-tech)
26 ___ Grande
27 Secret agent
29 What a volcano does
31 Closer to the color scarlet
34 Hard ___ rock: 2 words
36 How a French person would say "me"

39 Pain
41 Cable channel that shows sports: Abbreviation
42 What corn comes on
43 Thirteen minus twelve
44 Beginning for "night" or "west"
45 Bring ___ halt: 2 words
46 Group that finds out secrets for the government: Abbreviation
47 "On your mark, get ___, go!"

36

ACROSS

1 Unwell
4 Naughty
7 You might find one in your oatmeal
11 What you do to shoelaces
12 Feeling tender and achy
13 Continent that's next to Europe
14 ___ a bad example (be a poor role model)
15 Person in the White House
17 Skinny
19 Like winter roads, sometimes
20 The Pacific ___
22 Boat in the Bible
23 Go to ___ (hit the sack)
26 Harrison ___ (famous actor)
27 Ending for "lemon"
28 Part of a book
29 Billboards, for example
30 "Green Eggs ___ Ham"
31 Hair that comes down over your forehead
32 Liquid that people write with
33 State between Minnesota and Missouri

34 The wife of 15-Across: 2 words
38 Catch forty winks
41 Baker's need
42 December 24 and December 31, for example
43 Had a feast
44 The cost of living in an apartment
45 The Baltic ___ (body of water)
46 Tool that has teeth

DOWN

1 "Virtue is ___ own reward"
2 Be dishonest
3 Parts of the alphabet
4 "I wasn't ___ yesterday!" ("I'm not that gullible!")
5 "Who ___ you?"
6 Really want
7 Tramp's love, in a Disney movie
8 Take advantage of
9 One sixtieth of an hour: Abbreviation
10 ___ Sajak (host of "Wheel of Fortune")

12 Rotate
16 "Ugh, how disgusting!"
18 "Mary ___ a little lamb"
20 At the drop ___ hat (immediately): 2 words
21 Kind of fish
22 Do some arithmetic
23 Yellow fruits
24 Food in an omelet
25 ___ Moines (capital of 33-Across)
27 Leg joints
28 Hound's foot
30 Word that can go in front of "hill" or "farm"

31 ___ and girls
32 "___ that something!" ("That's impressive!")
33 "Hey, what's the big ___?"
34 "You asked ___ it!"
35 "Now ___ seen it all!"
36 Dog in an old TV cartoon series
37 5th ___ (chocolate candy bar)
39 "I'm ___ loss for words": 2 words
40 Place for people to sit in church

37

ACROSS

1 ___ talk (what a coach gives his players when they're losing)
4 Beginning for "fortune" or "understanding"
7 Kind of energy that comes from the sun
12 Canoeing need
13 Card without a number or a face on it
14 Leader, to Webelos scouts
15 Major-league athlete
16 "Not ___" ("Keep waiting")
17 Pig ___ (code that changes "puzzle" into "uzzlepay")
18 Letters before P
20 What breakfast in bed is served on
22 Pakistan's continent
24 "To ___ it may concern" (start of some letters)
25 Pekoe is this kind of drink
28 Chore that you might have to do after dinner: 3 words
31 Private ___ (detective)
32 "Darn it!"

33 The Incredible ___ (green superhero)
34 Bread that has a pocket in it
35 What someone uses to make calligraphy
36 Seat belt, for example
39 Frightening sound
41 Use a shovel
44 "Where there's ___, there's a way": 2 words
45 ___ down (get into bed)
46 According to the Bible, she was made out of Adam's rib
47 Large deer
48 Kind of tree
49 Bread used in a Reuben sandwich

DOWN

1 "Hop on ___" (Dr. Seuss book)
2 Hearing organ
3 Vow
4 Sandwich spread, for short
5 ___ skating
6 Chore that you might have to do before dinner: 3 words

7 Salty meat used in some sandwiches
8 Not too bad
9 Give permission to
10 ___ Baba
11 Took part in a footrace
19 Opposite of "yeah"
21 Fishing poles
22 In ___ of (amazed by)
23 Utter
24 "___ happened?"
25 Noise during a rainstorm
26 Fish that's hard to catch
27 Have a question

29 Three-base hit, in baseball
30 Not "he"
34 Friends
35 Something that rhymes
36 Uncle ___ (symbol of the United States)
37 Half of four
38 ___ de Janeiro (big Brazilian city)
40 It shoots out of a well in the ground
42 Plant that can grow on walls
43 "___ whiz!"

38

ACROSS

1 Room where Dr. Frankenstein worked
4 Elementary-school group: Abbreviation
7 Rock and Roll ___ of Fame (museum in Cleveland)
11 The Ice ___ (when glaciers covered the Earth)
12 One of the tokens in Monopoly
13 Dog that lives with Garfield
14 Letters that form an emergency signal
15 Insect with lots of legs
17 Those folks
19 Tool that fights weeds in a garden
20 Identical
22 Do some needlework
23 Health ___ (place where people try to get in shape)
26 Insect that looks like it's being religious: 2 words
30 Money that's used in Tokyo
31 Little baby
32 Pull hard
33 Cry
34 Big jungle animals

36 Insect that often gets killed by an exterminator
40 "For ___ a jolly good fellow ..."
43 "___ in a Manger" (Christmas song)
44 Changed the color of one's hair
45 How to stop being hungry
46 Dogs, cats, fish, and so on
47 "I agree"
48 ___ off (use a towel)

DOWN

1 ___ Vegas
2 Long ___ (many years back)
3 He stands next to the groom during the wedding: 2 words
4 Animal that's chased by another animal
5 Very heavy weight
6 National ___ (official song of a country)
7 Wish
8 Suffix in some drink names
9 It's on top of a jar
10 General Robert E. ___
12 ___ cream
16 State in the Midwest

18 "___, you!" ("I'm trying to get your attention")
20 Someone who tries to find out secrets
21 "How ___ you?"
22 Snorkel's rank, in "Beetle Bailey": Abbreviation
23 Stuck into storage
24 Safety ___ (fastening device)
25 Try to get an answer
27 "Believe ___ not!": 2 words
28 Not a single person
29 "Bill ___, the Science Guy" (TV show)

33 "The ___ the limit!"
34 There are four of them in a deck
35 Degree that a graduate student might get: Abbreviation
36 ___ gun (toy that shoots blanks)
37 "You ___ me one" ("I'll ask you for a favor back later")
38 Animal that purrs
39 How a sailor says "yes"
41 Have an ___ for music (have musical talent)
42 Place for a piglet

39

ACROSS

1 Birthday present
5 Something horses eat
8 Stay ___ (don't move)
11 "___ Want for Christmas Is My Two Front Teeth": 2 words
12 President's "no" on a bill from Congress
13 High ___ kite: 2 words
14 Kind of pie
16 Trash ___
17 The nearest star to the Earth
18 New ___ City
20 Miami's state: Abbreviation
23 Steal from
25 Deserve
28 Kind of pie: 2 words
32 "Give it ___ best shot"
33 The best score for an Olympic gymnast
34 What a chicken lays
35 ___ belt (strap in a car)
38 Chowed down
40 Piece of winter sports equipment
42 Kind of pie
47 Rooster's wife
48 Not poor

49 "Dear ___" (how some letters begin)
50 Country ruled by Queen Elizabeth II: Abbreviation
51 Ending for "absorb"
52 Fix an article before it gets printed

DOWN

1 The gift of ___ (ability to talk well)
2 Not healthy
3 Infectious disease
4 Makes a knot
5 That girl
6 "Give it ___!" ("Do your best"): 2 words
7 Toy that goes up and down: Hyphenated
8 Bundle that's wrapped up
9 Neighbor of Mexico: Abbreviation
10 Light brown color
12 The poison that comes from a snake
15 Set fire to
19 ___ and Stimpy (cartoon duo)

20 Ride in an airplane
21 Summertime zodiac sign
22 Funny
24 Make a wager
26 It covers part of a floor
27 Opposite of "positive": Abbreviation
29 Metal, when it's just been dug up
30 Get to
31 Vanish ___ thin air
36 Measure of land
37 Not fat

39 Something ___ (an additional thing)
40 "___ Loves You" (Beatles song)
41 ___ Griffey Jr. (famous baseball player)
43 Columbus Day is in this month: Abbreviation
44 Band-___ (scrape covering)
45 It can come before "pod" or "cycle"
46 At the end of a word, it means "most"

ACROSS

1 "Don't look ___ like that": 2 words
5 Blind as ___: 2 words
9 Kind of coat that some people object to
12 Line that goes up the side of a pair of pants
13 Wealthy
14 "Four-and-twenty blackbirds baked ___ pie": 2 words
15 Muppet on "Sesame Street": 3 words
18 Remains of a fire
19 "Japan" suffix
20 Baseball player's hat
23 Embrace
25 "The King of Rock and Roll"
29 Its capital is Salt Lake City
31 Ham on ___ (kind of sandwich)
33 What comes out of a volcano
34 10 degrees ___ zero (very cold)
36 "As I was going to St. Ives, I ___ a man with seven wives"
38 ___ Jersey
39 Old horse
41 "What do ___ want?"

43 Muppet on "Sesame Street": 2 words
50 Franks ___ beans
51 Celebrity
52 Song for one person
53 ___ Rover (playground game)
54 Masking ___
55 You can travel down a river on one

DOWN

1 "Go ___ your mother"
2 Golf ball's resting place
3 February follower: Abbreviation
4 ___ Watson (actress who played Hermione in "Harry Potter and the Sorcerer's Stone")
5 Cartoon about a young aardvark
6 A little ___ (small amount)
7 Feeling of pain
8 One of ___ days (sometime soon)
9 Kind of tree
10 Número ___ (#1, in Spanish)
11 Cloth used for dusting

16 Ending for "child" or "devil"

17 Tripped

20 Baby bear

21 Pigged out

22 Pen ___ (faraway person you write to)

24 Place to work out

26 Vehicle that people use when they move to a new house

27 "___ been thinking ..."

28 Observed

30 Squeeze a horn

32 Donkey in "Winnie-the-Pooh"

35 The middle of the body

37 2000 pounds

40 "___ load of this!" ("Watch!"): 2 words

42 Moscow was once its capital: Abbreviation

43 Sedan, for example

44 "We're number ___!"

45 Like the number 33

46 It shows you how to get around

47 Come ___ decision: 2 words

48 Keebler worker, in its commercials

49 Go bad

ANSWERS

1

C	U	B	A		T	H	A	W		G	O	O
A	S	I	N		A	U	T	O		E	A	R
B	A	L	D		T	H	E	O	D	O	R	E
		L	A	P				F	O	R		
D	O	C		E	A	S	T		I	G	O	R
I	L	L		A	L	O	H	A		E	W	E
E	D	I	T		A	B	E	L		W	E	D
		N	O	W				L	A	B		
C	A	T	W	O	M	A	N		B	U	L	B
A	G	O		R	O	S	E		A	S	I	A
P	E	N		M	E	A	T		T	H	E	Y

2

S	A	T		N	A	S	A		C	A	N	S
A	R	E		I	T	I	S		O	P	I	E
L	I	E		P	A	R	K	P	L	A	C	E
S	E	N	D	S				E	A	R	E	D
A	L	S	O		S	O	D	A		T	R	Y
			C	H	I	N	E	S	E			
L	A	P		A	P	E	S		A	C	E	S
A	L	L	A	N				S	T	R	A	P
B	O	A	R	D	W	A	L	K		U	S	E
O	N	I	T		O	B	E	Y		D	E	C
R	E	D	S		N	E	T	S		E	L	K

3

C	A	P	E	S		H	A	S		J	A	M
A	B	E	L	L		I	C	Y		A	G	O
P	E	P	S	I		S	I	R		W	E	B
		P	E	P	E		D	U	M	B		
T	O	E		S	A	D		P	U	R	S	E
E	A	R	S		T	O	O		D	E	A	L
A	R	M	O	R		E	L	F		A	T	M
			I	S	E	E		D	E	S	K	
P	A	N		A	R	K		N	E	E	D	S
A	C	T		D	I	E		C	A	R	O	L
Y	E	S		Y	E	N		E	S	S	A	Y

4

A	G	E	S		C	A	R		P	A	T	S
M	E	E	T		U	S	E		I	D	E	A
A	T	L	A	N	T	I	C	O	C	E	A	N
			T	O	E		I	N	K			
F	I	R	E	D		A	P	E		M	A	Y
A	C	E	S		P	I	E		G	A	T	E
N	E	D		J	A	R		P	A	N	E	S
			H	E	S		F	U	R			
G	R	E	A	T	S	A	L	T	L	A	K	E
A	I	N	T		E	V	E		I	R	I	S
P	O	D	S		S	E	A		C	E	N	T

5

M	A	R	S		T	A	P	S		B	U	M
A	L	O	T		A	S	I	A		A	S	A
D	A	T	E		T	H	E	L	O	R	A	X
			M	A	T		D	E	N			
N	A	N		N	O	T		C	A	P	S	
O	N	B	E	Y	O	N	D	Z	E	B	R	A
S	N	A	G			T	E	A		C	O	W
			G	A	S		E	G	O			
H	O	P	O	N	P	O	P		P	E	P	E
E	W	E		T	O	N	E		E	V	E	N
N	E	T		S	T	A	R		N	E	R	D

6

S	T	A	B		L	E	I		A	H	A
T	O	B	E		J	O	L	T		L	O	G
A	B	I	T		U	S	E	S		O	N	E
G	E	T	S	I	N		M	A	S	H	E	D
E	Y	E		L	I	M	E		H	A	Y	
			C	L	O	O	N	E	Y			
	S	A	D		R	O	T	S		W	E	T
J	O	S	E	P	H		A	P	P	E	A	R
E	L	K		L	I	A	R		R	A	T	E
E	V	E		U	G	L	Y		O	V	E	N
R	E	D		S	H	E		M	E	N	D	

7

P	A	W		J	I	L	L		L	O	G	S
U	S	A		O	D	I	E		I	S	E	E
P	A	R	A	K	E	E	T		S	T	E	W
			P	E	A		T	E	A	R		
T	A	P	E			N	E	V		I	D	O
I	C	E		A	W	A	R	E		C	O	N
P	E	N		L	A	P			S	H	O	E
		G	O	L	F		T	I	C			
S	P	U	N		F	L	A	M	I	N	G	O
E	R	I	C		L	A	M	P		B	O	W
T	O	N	E		E	Y	E	S		A	T	E

8

B	A	R	E		S	P	Y		Z	A	P	
A	P	E	S		T	O	O		I	N	A	
H	U	M	P	T	Y	D	U	M	P	T	Y	
			N	H	L		R	A	P			
M	O	O		E	E	K		P	E	C	A	N
R	I	N	G		S	I	T		R	A	C	E
S	L	E	E	T		D	I	D		P	E	T
		Y	E	S		N	O	T				
	S	E	S	A	M	E	S	T	R	E	E	T
I	V	E		O	W	E		A	M	A	N	
P	E	R		G	E	L		P	U	T	T	

9

L	A	Y		M	E	S	S		I	W	A	S
I	T	O		A	L	O	T		T	I	L	E
S	O	S		D	O	M	E		S	L	O	P
A	M	E	N		P	E	A	R		E	A	T
	S	M	I	L	E		M	O	O	E	D	
		I	C	E				A	B	C		
	S	T	E	A	K		B	R	O	O	M	
A	P	E		F	I	N	E		E	Y	E	S
S	O	S	O		T	O	R	E		O	L	E
I	R	A	N		E	W	E	S		T	O	N
A	T	M	E		S	I	T	S		E	N	D

10

T	W	O		S	H	E		L	A	S	E	R
E	E	L		P	A	N		A	L	I	V	E
N	E	D		A	N	D		T	I	M	E	D
		K	I	N	D		B	E	E	P		
T	H	I	N	K		B	A	R		L	A	B
H	O	N	K		Y	E	T		M	E	N	U
E	G	G		C	A	T		L	I	S	T	S
		C	O	R	K		T	A	X	I		
A	B	O	V	E		D	O	C		M	O	P
S	A	L	E	S		A	R	E		O	N	A
A	G	E	N	T		Y	E	S		N	E	W

11

S	A	W		S	P	A		A	C	T	E	D
A	L	A		C	A	B		L	O	O	S	E
D	I	S	N	E	Y	C	H	A	N	N	E	L
		H	E	N	S		A	R	E			
W	A	I	S	T		A	R	M		G	Y	M
I	S	N	T		L	I	E		D	E	E	R
T	A	G		T	A	R		P	A	N	T	S
		F	E	D		H	I	R	E			
C	O	M	E	D	Y	C	E	N	T	R	A	L
A	W	O	R	D		A	R	K		A	G	E
P	E	N	N	Y		T	O	Y		L	O	G

12

S	E	A	T		P	A	W	N		G	O	T
T	A	L	E		O	R	E	O		A	P	E
A	T	L	A	N	T	A	B	R	A	V	E	S
T	E	E		I	T	I	S		B	E	R	T
E	R	N		E	E	L		C	O	L	A	S
			V	C	R		P	A	Y			
A	G	R	E	E		C	A	R		C	A	P
S	O	O	T		P	O	R	E		A	D	O
H	O	U	S	T	O	N	A	S	T	R	O	S
E	S	T		A	G	E	D		H	E	R	E
S	E	E		N	O	S	E		E	Y	E	S

13

A	N	D	A		D	R	I	P		S	O	N
R	O	O	T		I	O	W	A		E	W	E
M	R	G	O	O	D	B	A	R		A	N	T
			M	A	Y		S	T	O	W		
I	A	M		T	O	E		Y	I	E	L	D
S	L	A	W		U	S	E		L	E	I	A
H	I	R	E	D		P	U	T		D	E	N
		B	E	E	F		R	O	O			
I	L	L		A	L	M	O	N	D	J	O	Y
T	E	E		L	E	A	P		D	O	N	E
S	O	S		S	A	N	E		S	E	E	S

14

H	I	D	E	S		A	D	S		P	O	D
A	S	I	D	E		L	E	T		E	A	R
S	T	A	G	E		L	E	E		T	R	Y
		N	E	D	S		P	A	G	E		
I	N	A		S	A	W		L	A	R	G	E
T	O	P	S		T	I	P		S	P	I	N
S	T	R	A	W		N	O	W		A	N	D
		I	D	E	A		P	O	O	R		
P	A	N		I	S	A		R	A	K	E	S
E	T	C		R	I	D		S	T	E	V	E
G	E	E		D	A	D		T	H	R	E	W

15

F	A	S	T		A	M	P	S		T	A	P
U	T	A	H		R	O	O	T		U	S	E
R	E	N	O		C	O	L	U	M	B	I	A
		T	U	B	A		O	N	A			
B	A	A		A	D	S		P	O	P	S	
E	L	F		T	E	A	R	S		L	I	E
D	E	E	P		T	E	E		Y	E	T	
			R	S	T		F	A	R	M		
H	O	N	O	L	U	L	U		U	P	T	O
A	R	E		O	N	E	S		T	I	E	D
D	E	W		P	A	G	E		H	A	N	D

16

L	E	F	T	A		J	E	T		P	A	D
A	A	R	O	N		A	L	A		T	I	E
B	R	I	T	N	E	Y	S	P	E	A	R	S
			S	O	Y		E	E	L			
B	O	A		Y	E	S		S	M	A	R	T
E	A	S	T		S	A	D		O	D	I	E
D	R	A	W	S		T	E	A		S	O	N
			I	M	A		E	T	C			
J	E	N	N	I	F	E	R	L	O	P	E	Z
A	V	E		T	R	A		A	R	O	M	A
W	E	T		H	O	T		S	E	T	U	P

17

T	I	S		O	F	F		P	A	S	T	A
I	N	K		R	O	O		A	C	H	E	D
M	A	I	L	B	O	X		I	R	O	N	S
			A	I	D		F	R	E	E		
W	A	S	N	T		B	U	S		B	A	A
A	B	A	D		P	E	N		F	O	R	D
R	U	N		T	I	E		M	I	X	E	D
		D	A	R	E		F	O	R			
C	A	B	L	E		B	O	O	M	B	O	X
A	B	O	V	E		O	L	D		A	N	Y
T	E	X	A	S		O	K	S		T	A	Z

18

P	A	T	S		T	A	L	L		S	A	P
A	B	E	E		I	D	E	A		O	L	E
L	O	N	E		M	E	O	W		C	I	A
M	O	N	K	S				N	I	C	E	R
S	K	I		H	O	S	T		D	E	N	S
		S	P	E	C	T	A	T	O	R		
P	A	C	E		T	Y	P	O		F	I	N
A	L	O	N	E				M	A	I	N	E
S	T	U		C	L	A	M		L	E	G	S
T	A	R		H	A	R	E		S	L	O	T
A	R	T		O	P	E	N		O	D	D	S

19

S	N	O	B		C	A	S	H		P	A	C
H	O	N	I		A	R	E	A		A	L	L
A	T	I	T		M	I	L	L		R	I	O
F	R	O	S	T	E	D	F	L	A	K	E	S
T	E	N		O	R	E			M	A	N	E
			P	E	A		S	T	Y			
A	L	S	O			A	T	E		B	E	A
G	O	L	D	E	N	G	R	A	H	A	M	S
O	W	E		G	O	R	E		I	T	C	H
N	E	D		G	O	E	S		T	H	E	E
Y	R	S		O	N	E	S		S	E	E	S

20

I	L	L		S	A	N		O	R	A	L
S	E	A	T		E	C	O		P	O	G	O
H	O	G	W	A	R	T	S		E	W	E	S
		O	W	E		E	A	R	L			
I	A	M		A	N	T		N	A	I	L	S
F	L	U		K	A	R	A	T		N	O	T
A	L	G	A	E		A	S	H		G	U	Y
	G	U	S	T			T	E	A			
C	O	L	D		H	E	R	M	I	O	N	E
O	N	E	I		A	G	O		R	U	B	S
P	A	S	O		N	O	S		T	A	P	

21

	B	A	B	E		R	O	T		A	T	A
	O	I	L	S		I	D	O		L	E	D
	G	L	A	S	S	B	O	T	T	L	E	S
		B	A	T		R	E	Y				
A	S	A		Y	E	T		S	P	A	T	S
N	E	X	T		P	A	W		E	C	H	O
D	W	E	E	B		P	A	D		T	E	N
		A	R	K		R	E	D				
A	L	U	M	I	N	U	M	C	A	N	S	
R	A	N		D	O	S		K	N	E	E	
T	W	O		E	W	E		S	E	T	A	

22

S	L	A	M		B	A	C	K				
L	A	L	A		A	C	H	E		W	A	X
A	N	A	P		B	E	A	N		R	U	M
P	E	R		E	A	S	T		N	I	T	E
	S	M	E	A	R		S	E	A	S	O	N
		C	D	S				A	N	T		
A	L	L	E	Y	S		D	R	A	W	S	
L	I	O	N		C	A	R	S		A	C	T
I	N	C		R	O	P	E		S	T	A	R
E	E	K		I	R	I	S		A	C	R	E
			P	E	G	S		W	H	E	E	

23

C	O	A	S	T		A	C	T		D	I	M
O	R	D	E	R		B	O	Y		O	F	A
T	E	M	P	O		C	A	P	T	A	I	N
		I	T	U	P		T	E	A			
F	A	R		T	A	N		D	I	G	I	T
I	R	A	N		L	O	W		L	E	N	O
B	E	L	O	W		D	A	M		N	A	P
		N	E	T		R	A	C	E			
C	O	L	O	N	E	L		R	U	R	A	L
O	N	E		D	A	B		S	T	A	L	E
W	A	G		Y	R	S		H	E	L	L	O

24

A	T	M		T	H	I	S		R	A	S	H
B	O	O		H	A	L	T		A	S	I	A
U	M	B	R	E	L	L	A		Z	A	N	Y
		O	Y	L		I	D	O				
C	L	A	W			S	N	O	R	K	E	L
O	I	L		S	M	A	S	H		I	T	E
B	L	A	N	K	E	T		O	N	C	E	
		A	I	S		S	A	W				
I	T	E	M		S	U	N	B	L	O	C	K
S	A	V	E		E	P	I	C		D	U	E
A	X	E	S		S	A	P	S		D	E	N

90

25

26

27

28

29

30

31

```
S E E D S   E S P   L A W
A W A I T   A T A   O N E
P E T E R   R A P   B Y E
      T A P   R A G S
S N O   W O O F   I T S A
T A C O   R B I   N E L L
U P T O   P I S A   R Y E
      O H I O   H I T
O O P   R I P   S W A P S
F L U   A S A   L I M I T
A D S   N E W   E X I T S
```

32

```
T A C   S H A P E   P R O
A G O   P O S E D   R E D
P E N   A M A Z E   E N D
      J A N E   N A P
P A U L   R I P   D O T S
I S N T   U F O   A S I A
N I C E   N I P   M I N D
      T R Y   C O S T
T R I   A D D O N   I A M
W O O   M O O R E   O R E
O W N   S C A N S   N E T
```

33

```
L A T E   F E D   A T E
I M A C S   L E E   N O W
L I G H T B U L B   D Y E
      O E R   S T A R
A R T   R A P   S O O N
S E W I N G M A C H I N E
A X I S   S I R   D A W
      S A S H   R O W
H A T   T E L E P H O N E
I C E   A R E   S I N U S
P E R   B E T   P E T S
```

34

```
      L E S S   B E G S
C U T   A R U T   O R E O
A S I   P A I R   B E N D
P E N S   S T A G   C I A
  S K A T E   W R I T E S
    E Y E     I D O
T Y R A N T   S T E R N
R A T   T H A W   A S I A
A H O Y   A L O T   E N G
Y O Y O   T I R E   T E E
S O S O   S E E N
```

35

```
  W I N   G O D   C L A P
  A C E   A L I   L A T E
  R E C O R D P L A Y E R
      K I D   S A W
P A R   L E D   W E A R S
E R I E   N O R   D R I P
Z E B R A   G E M   T O Y
      U S A   D O E
C O M P A C T D I S C S
O N I T   H O E   P I E
B E D S   E A R   N A T
```

36

```
I L L   B A D   L U M P
T I E   S O R E   A S I A
S E T   P R E S I D E N T
    T H I N   I C Y
O C E A N   A R K   B E D
F O R D   A D E   P A G E
A D S   A N D   B A N G S
      I N K   I O W A
F I R S T L A D Y   N A P
O V E N   E V E S   A T E
R E N T   S E A   S A W
```

37

```
P E P   M I S   S O L A R
O A R   A C E   A K E L A
P R O   Y E T   L A T I N
      M N O   T R A Y
A S I A   W H O M   T E A
W A S H T H E D I S H E S
E Y E   R A T S   H U L K
      P I T A   P E N
S T R A P   B O O   D I G
A W I L L   L I E   E V E
M O O S E   E L M   R Y E
```

38

```
L A B   P T A   H A L L
A G E   I R O N   O D I E
S O S   C E N T I P E D E
      T H E Y   H O E
S A M E   S E W   S P A
P R A Y I N G M A N T I S
Y E N   T O T   Y A N K
      S O B   A P E S
C O C K R O A C H   H E S
A W A Y   D Y E D   E A T
P E T S   Y E S   D R Y
```

39

```
G I F T   H A Y   P U T
A L L I   V E T O   A S A
B L U E B E R R Y   C A N
      S U N   Y O R K
F L A   R O B     E A R N
L E M O N M E R I N G U E
Y O U R   T E N   E G G
      S E A T   A T E
S K I   C H O C O L A T E
H E N   R I C H   S I R S
E N G   E N T   E D I T
```

40

```
A T M E   A B A T   F U R
S E A M   R I C H   I N A
K E R M I T T H E F R O G
      A S H   E S E
C A P   H U G   E L V I S
U T A H   R Y E   L A V A
B E L O W   M E T   N E W
      N A G   Y O U
C O O K I E M O N S T E R
A N D   S T A R   S O L O
R E D   T A P E   R A F T
```

ABOUT THE AUTHOR

Trip Payne's first published crossword was in the Chapman Elementary School newspaper when he was in the fourth grade. He kept on making puzzles, and now he's a professional puzzlemaker living in Atlanta. Aside from the *Crosswords for Kids* series, he has made kids' puzzles for such publications as *Scholastic News*, *Games Junior*, and *Zigzag*.

Dan Wenke at Bern-Art Studios

ALSO BY TRIP PAYNE

Amazing Crosswords for Kids
Sterling ISBN 978-1-4027-1039-1

Awesome Crosswords for Kids
Sterling ISBN 978-1-4027-1038-4

Challenging Crosswords for Kids
Sterling ISBN 978-1-4027-0555-7

Clever Crosswords for Kids
978-1-4027-0556-4

Crosswords for Kids
Sterling ISBN 978-0-8069-1249-3

Fantastically Fun Crosswords for Kids
Sterling ISBN 978-1-4027-2163-2

Super Crosswords for Kids
Sterling ISBN 978-0-8069-9290-7

Trivial Pursuit for Kids Crosswords
Sterling ISBN 978-1-4027-5154-7